SET FOR
LIFE

SET FOR LIFE

*Dominate Life,
Money, and
the American Dream*

By Scott Trench

BiggerPockets
PUBLISHING

Set For Life: Dominate Life, Money and the American Dream
Scott Trench

Published by BiggerPockets Publishing LLC, Denver, CO
Hardcover Edition Copyright © 2017 by Scott Trench
Paperback Edition Copyright © 2019 by Scott Trench
All Rights Reserved.

Publisher's Cataloging-in-Publication Data

Names: Trench, Scott, author.

Title: Set for life : dominate life , money , and the American dream / by Scott Trench.

Description: Denver, CO: BiggerPockets Publishing, LLC, 2019.

Identifiers: ISBN 9780997584714 (Hardcover) | 9781947200180 (pbk.) | 978-0-9975847-2-1 (ebook)

Subjects: LCSH Finance, Personal. | Investments. | Real estate investment. | Rental housing. | Self-actualization (Psychology) | Quality of life. | BISAC BUSINESS & ECONOMICS / Personal Finance / General | BUSINESS & ECONOMICS / Real Estate / General

Classification: LCC HG179 .T74 2017 | DDC 332.024--dc23

Printed in the United States of America
10 9 8 7 6 5 4 3 2 1

Contents

Introduction

Let's talk about the American Dream. Traditionally, for the majority of us— at least for those of us in the middle class—it means consistency. It means buying a nice home, in a nice neighborhood, and having a nice life. It means that after a thirty or forty-year career, we plan to retire using a formula that historically hinges on having saved 10 to 15 percent of our income and having invested in a 401(k) or other retirement vehicle.

The problem with this formula is that the working person following it will be forced to work for wage income for the better part of his day, during the best part of his week, throughout the best years of his life. At best, he will retire with a modest amount of wealth, late in life, and be forced to hope it's enough to last.

How about a different formula for the American Dream? How about something capable of producing a retirement level of wealth in less than ten years? How about less than five? How about retiring in your twenties from wage-paying work?

Those who accomplish this financial result can laugh off would-be employers who ask them to be at work before 9:00 a.m. She can spend a sunny summer Tuesday at the park instead of crunching spreadsheets in a dusty cubicle. He can stay up until 3:00 a.m. binge-watching *Game of Thrones* on Sunday night, and head to the gym at noon on Monday. She can rent out her house and travel the world, living like a local. He can start a business funded with passive income, volunteer in his community, or focus on raising his small children. She can serve others without the red tape and bureaucracy of corporate involvement or the interference of a boss with objectives different from hers.

Early financial freedom enables this. Those who achieve early financial freedom build wealth and acquire assets such that they produce passive income in excess of what they need to live. And they expect to continue

1

to generate that level of income for the duration of their lives. Regardless of whether you currently enjoy your work or not, early financial freedom is a worthwhile goal. Industries change, companies change, and coworkers change. Even if you love your job, wouldn't it be great to have the *option* to leave wage-paying work? Wouldn't it be great to know that you show up because you love to be there, and not because you have to be there?

This book will teach you how to make wage income irrelevant to your financial picture in just a few years. In this book, you will learn how to re-design your lifestyle, restart your career, and rebuild your financial position. In this book, you will save your money, earn more money, and use the cash you accumulate to purchase freedom and the ability to design your day-to-day life without the need for wage-paying work. This book is designed for someone with a specific set of circumstances. It is designed for the full-time median (around $50,000 per year) wage earner who has little to no initial savings but wants early financial freedom.

Three Stages of Wealth Creation

This book offers a simple, three-step approach to gaining early financial freedom. It is written with a specific audience in mind: the full-time wage earner starting with little to no wealth but aspiring to early financial freedom. Each step in the journey increases one's flexibility and exposes the individual to more and more opportunities. Each step increases one's *financial runway*—the number of years that one can maintain their lifestyle without the need for wage-paying work. Many Americans can't survive for more than a few months without earning a paycheck. Readers of this book will rapidly develop a financial position capable of sustaining their lives for a year without work. Then they'll extend their financial runway to five years. Then forever.

Part I of this book will take Average Joe from $0 to $25,000 in personal wealth. You have to start somewhere, and the median wage earner with little to no accessible wealth will begin their journey by focusing on lifestyle design. Part I teaches readers how to make the necessary changes to go from little to no savings to preserving over 50 percent of one's middle class income. It teaches readers how to live well on less than $2000 per month and how to use the savings to pay down debt and extend their financial runway to a year or more. Executing this leaves the reader in a position to have a full year of expenses in after-tax wealth, ready to be deployed in pursuit of early financial freedom.

Part II of this book takes readers from $25,000 to $100,000 in personal wealth. It takes readers from one year of financial runway to a position in which they could survive for three to five years or more without earning a paycheck. While continuing to live efficient lifestyles, readers will further reduce their living expenses by purchasing a primary residence that allows them to live for free. They will also learn how to earn significantly more income by changing careers and how to develop habits tied to success. Opportunities to earn more income often develop out of careers in sales or technology, or are the result of joining a small company or freelancing. The financial runway developed in Part I will be critical to ensuring that readers can pursue these opportunities with little risk.

Part III of this book takes readers from $100,000 to early financial freedom. It takes them from several years of financial runway to a lifetime of permanent financial abundance. Readers will continue to scale their income and live efficiently, but our focus shifts to the purchase and creation of income-producing assets. Readers are exposed to an advanced discussion on the concept of financial freedom and taught investment philosophy. They learn what types of wealth count toward financial freedom, and what types don't. This background will enable readers to intelligently exploit the investment and income opportunities multiplying before them as their financial position improves and their financial runway lengthens. Readers also learn how to track their progress efficiently.

This book layers philosophy alongside practical knowledge. Wealth creation is not a rigid formula or step-by-step process. Don't ignore income opportunities while you focus on building your first $25,000. Don't ignore investment opportunities while accumulating the first $100,000. You need to earn more, spend less, and invest the difference aggressively throughout your journey, as they apply to the specifics of your situation.

Understand that accumulating a lifetime of wealth in a short period of time involves making personal decisions in major areas of your life that are different from the norm. It involves working harder and smarter than the average employee, and it involves making different career decisions than the Average Joe. Achieving early financial freedom involves managing wealth in a totally different way. In short, it involves a change of perspective that may be sharply at odds from that of your family, friends, and colleagues.

Examples of the perspective you're about to discover include:
- You should start by saving the next $1000, not earning the next $1000.

- A new car is totally unnecessary.

- You should spend more, not less, on entertainment and fun.

- Student loan debt is rarely worth it.

- Buying a home (or worse, a condo) in the best part of town will slow you down on your path to early financial freedom.

- Stocks are less risky than bonds.

- You need to spend less money to earn more money.

- Developing a specialty is far more risky than being a jack-of-all-trades.

- A few good options are better than too many options.

- Contribute less, not more, to your retirement accounts—and be ready to withdraw from them early.

If you want a different financial result, you need a different plan. This book offers that plan. Work hard. Spend as little as possible. Invest the difference intelligently. Set yourself up for life, as early as you possibly can. No, it's not easy. It will be up to you to decide if it's worth it.

Part I
The First $25,000 Is the Hardest

This section shows you how to put yourself in a position where you have over a year of financial runway. It teaches you how to accumulate your first meaningful amount of capital. You will do this by focusing heavily on the preservation of your median income, and by cutting out spending where it will make the most impact. To achieve the goal of this section, you need to accumulate at least one year of spending in readily accessible cash or cash equivalents.

Why should you do this? Because this runway buys you flexibility, freedom, and the ability to make your first big investment. This kind of wealth-building makes the next stage of wealth creation easy and automatic—and it will force you to think about building readily accessible wealth, not just maxing out a 401(k) or making a mortgage payment. You may not be able to retire forever on one year of savings, but you can certainly introduce yourself to a *wealth of choice*—the ability to take advantage of opportunities unavailable to those with weaker financial positions.

Remember, the goal is to build out a yearlong financial runway. Retirement savings, home equity, cars, and other false assets aren't useful to the individual who wishes to work toward early financial freedom. The fellow with $20,000 in retirement savings and $40,000 in home equity, but who spends $3000 per month and has just $7000 in the bank, has no financial runway. If he leaves his job, he runs out of cash in three months. Compare this to the guy with $25,000 in cold hard cash and a $2000 per month lifestyle. He can leave his job for a year or longer and be just fine. He can take advantage of opportunities unavailable to the first fellow. Why? Because the $25,000 is real. It is after-tax, and in the bank, and the guy who accumulated it is ready and willing to spend it to advance his position.

Be the guy with $25,000 in the bank and real options. Don't be the guy with just the mortgage and the 401(k) and no after-tax accessible wealth to show for it. The former can pursue his dreams and land on his feet if something goes wrong. The latter has no real wealth that he can deploy in the short term and is locked into working his current job or one very much like it to cover the mortgage.

For some folks, a year's worth of expenses will be $50,000 or more. That will change. After reading this section, you will know exactly what you need to do to put yourself in a position where your annual spending is well under $25,000 per year. You'll learn how to do this by cutting back on some big, unnecessary expenses in your budget that will free up both time and money.

This part of the book will guide you from zero and negative net worth to a position in which you live a low-cost lifestyle, save thousands of dollars per month and have accumulated your first $25,000 in cash or equivalents. It will also teach you how to live a happy, healthy, and fulfilling life on $2000 per month or less.

Uber after work. Or taking a second job on weekends.

Lifestyle design (frugality) can have a large impact for many full-time employed individuals seeking early financial freedom. It can be painlessly implemented, increase free time, and will definitely result in a large increase in monthly savings. And, while no one got rich through savings alone, efficient lifestyle design also *enables* the saver to start those other business and side-hustle ventures if that is how they choose to apply the savings and extra time they generate.

Reason #3: Our Tax System Favors the Saver, Not the Earner

Surprise! *Income* is taxed in the United States of America (and many other countries). That's *income*, not *wealth*.

Those in the demographic most likely to benefit from reading this book are probably paying a marginal tax of 30 to 35 percent on any income earned, including both state and federal taxes. And more earnings mean more taxes. A single person earning $50,000 per year who gets a 10 percent raise (a *really* large raise!) might think they are $5000 per year richer. But they are wrong. This person is really only making about $3300 per year more, after taxes take their bite out of the new income.

Instead, if this person just moved closer to work and into a slightly less expensive apartment, he or she might spend $5000 less per year between the commute and the rent. That's money they get to keep—they truly *are* $5000 per year richer. Furthermore, the move does not preclude this person from earning a raise—obviously it's great to get a raise. Understand, however, the absurdity of attempting to move toward financial freedom by working fifty to sixty-hour weeks for small percentage increases in taxable income when thousands of dollars in after-tax wealth can be easily saved!

Another way of stating this concept is to say that it's 33 percent more effective for someone in this tax bracket to save money than to attempt to earn it. A penny saved is 1.33 pennies earned!

In Summary

The preservation of capital should be the primary starting focus for financially ambitious nine-to-five employees for three main reasons:

- Frugality exposes the saver to opportunity.

- Frugality is noninvasive to one's lifestyle relative to moonlighting or building businesses.

- A penny saved is *better* than a penny earned because it is after-tax wealth.

This is not to discredit the importance of scaling your income and increasing your investment returns. This is just to point out that it's less effective to attempt to earn more money or invest efficiently when you can have far more impact by taking control of your spending. This does not mean that you should stop trying for that promotion at work! But it does mean that your focus starting out should be on saving more of your income, wherever and whenever practical.

Finance is more often than not a game of multiplication and exponential synergies. Folks that spend less can earn more. Investments that produce more cash flow can appreciate faster. You don't have to spend less and earn less. Spend less to earn more instead.

The Psychology of Frugality

The strategy outlined in this book relies heavily on your level of emotional motivation. None of the content will matter to you if you don't care about gaining early financial freedom. If you're perfectly happy working a forty-year career, or uninterested in planning your financial future, then becoming frugal and changing your lifestyle in the pursuit of early financial freedom will not be appealing. On the other hand, if the concept of early financial freedom strikes a chord, if you are convinced this should be your goal, then you will experience a powerful emotional urge to pursue this goal.

Early financial freedom should be a powerful motivator. The result of attaining financial freedom is a life lived on your terms. A life of impact. A life of growth. That motivation should be the driving force behind many of the most important financial decisions you make.

Your long-term goal should be one that is rooted in emotion. You must have great pride to work to become a champion athlete. You must have tremendous love to find a life partner. You must have great ambition to become a successful politician. And you must yearn for freedom to effectively pursue frugality as a means toward early financial freedom.

You may have noticed champion athletes don't let their emotions interfere with their focus in the arena. They don't train in bits and starts.

Successful politicians don't stay in the game long or successfully lead nations with wild emotional reactions to outside stimuli. And those who excel at personal finance don't make rash decisions with their money.

You must pursue a long-term goal based on your deep emotional desires. The strength of your desire to become financially free early in life is paramount to your success. But, you must also learn to control your emotions and moods in the short term. It's called being disciplined. Do not allow shallow, short-term emotions to prevent you from achieving your bigger goals. In the short term, emotions can be our enemies. Over the long term, they can be powerful allies.

This directly applies to disciplined spending. Just because tickets to the big game or a great concert are on sale, even at a great price, doesn't mean you should pounce on them. Instead, ask yourself the following question: *Is that event/trip/item so important that I'm willing to delay my financial freedom in order to purchase it?*

There's nothing wrong with saying "yes!" occasionally to the above question; nothing wrong with having fun and buying things that are awesome with your hard-earned money. But, always understand the implications of those purchases. Always understand just how far back they set you on your journey toward early financial freedom. You should become very uncomfortable spending money unnecessarily, because wanton spending delays your freedom.

A deep-rooted desire to attain early financial freedom makes decision-making on purchases more rational, and it makes living a frugal lifestyle far more achievable. For example, many people who attempt to take control of their spending rely heavily on budgets and other tools to remain disciplined. They might set aside $100 for clothing, $200 for meals out, and $150 for gas in any given month. They'll refer to these budgets when making financial decisions and use them to keep themselves on track. They do this because they want to be in command of the moment. They don't allow their short-term emotions and desires to get in the way of what they truly want.

However, you do not need to make budgets, and stick to them, or track every dollar every month of the year (we'll get to tracking things later on) if you aspire to the long-term goal of early financial freedom. If you consistently prioritize your early financial freedom the way it deserves to be prioritized, then many spending decisions are easy. For instance, you won't set aside any money for clothing, meals out, or gas. Instead, you will make decisions on a case-by-case basis, erring toward the lowest cost option to fulfill your needs and desires wherever reasonable. Tactics like budgeting can be useful, but they aren't critical. Far more impactful will be your emotional thirst to move toward early financial freedom. That desire will force you to make decisions logically based on an emotional desire, with or without a monthly budget.

Whether you want early financial freedom so you can focus on raising a family, pursuing a hobby, relaxing on the beach, traveling the world, or making an impact on your community, the reason you're working toward early financial freedom needs to be at the forefront when it comes to each individual spending decision. You need to prioritize the end goal more than you prioritize trinkets and luxuries. Your long-term motivation needs to be stronger than the vast majority of your short-term urges.

Get Rich by Doing It Yourself

One of the fallacies many people have is the idea they need to turn to the "experts" in order to do basic things to run their lives. Americans tend to rely on professionals in increasingly alarming ways:

- They blindly follow their medical doctor's advice.
- They expect therapists and psychiatrists to help them through mental and emotional problems.
- They helplessly rely on mechanics to keep their cars running.
- They hire plumbers to fix basic water problems.
- They fearfully ask lawyers to watch over every legal loophole.
- They blindly trust financial advisors to handle their money.
- They ignorantly hope for accountants to file their taxes correctly.

Professionals and specialists have their place. It's absolutely critical to go see a doctor for a broken bone, a psychiatrist for dark or violent thoughts, and to rely on specialists for specific problems that might have negative consequences. However, it's not the doctor's job to keep you healthy. It is your job to do that. You need to study exercise and physical strength training to keep your body fit. You need to figure out what foods are healthy and unhealthy. You need to make sure you are getting the sleep you need to be happy, healthy, and productive. You go to the doctor for emergent problems and checkups, and to see if there's anything you might have missed.

It's also not the plumber's job to fix your toilet. It's your job to do that. Toilets are extremely rudimentary pieces of equipment and anyone reading this book is capable of watching a few YouTube videos showing how to diagnose, repair, and safely replace a toilet in a few hours. It is the plumber's job to fix problems that are beyond the scope of simple repair work. Likewise, it is not necessarily the psychiatrist's job to solve every problem you have with your family. You need to proactively work through a bad day, a relationship problem, and internal struggles. If you want to expedite financial freedom, you must become reasonably competent in solving day-to-day problems and fixing things yourself.

Don't be a coward. Part of life, and part of becoming wealthy is taking responsibility for your life. Learning how to manage the important things in your life (your home, your equipment, your body, your mind, and your car) is part of that process. Yes, you will screw up a few things. The sink might drip for a few weeks until you replace the drain, or you might make a mess when first trying to change your oil. Across any one individual job, you increase your risk of problems associated with work when you don't hire it out to an expert. But, if you fear trivial failures to the point where you outsource basic tasks to professionals you will almost certainly lose out on opportunities to grow over the long run.

Instead, attempt at first to do things yourself. Develop an understanding of the scope of work involved and the potential risks to look out for. Then, make a decision about hiring out the work. Do not hire out tasks unless one of the following is true:

- There are potentially catastrophic consequences of misdiagnosing the problem. Think of this like a broken bone, suspicious lump, or other chronic health issue that doesn't go away after a few nights of sound sleep and a few intense exercise sessions.

- It is unlikely the job can be completed in less than one full business day, and the job needs to be done as soon as possible.

- There are issues with completing the work that might create unreasonable liability (for example, it may be unwise to do electrical work on a rental property, because insurance might not cover any problems associated with that work).

- You've previously performed similar work, can safely say that you particularly detest the work, and can pay someone else to do the work for less than $25 per hour.

There are idiots in every single profession, and frankly, some "licensed" professionals can actually give you advice that's wrong or downright dangerous. It does not make sense to go to a real estate agent located in Denver, Colorado and ask their opinion on the market in New York City. It's just as ridiculous to go to a lawyer who specializes in patent law and ask his opinion on a rental lease. The same goes for talking to an accountant who audits large companies and asking her to prepare your individual return. These industries are so broad, that finding a professional who is uniquely suited to solving your specific problems is a challenge unto itself. Do not look for expensive professional advice without doing at least a few hours of in-depth research on the subject to find someone who fits the bill.

You might be surprised at how quickly you can learn about legal concepts. Why not seek legal help only after you have reviewed the issues and understand exactly what you need help with, both broadly and down to specific issues? Likewise, it makes little sense to hire a financial advisor if you have no idea how to manage money. Instead, first learn about investing, and then hire a financial planner only if you think he or she can do it better than you. Why would you hire any old financial advisor, especially if said advisor is incapable of saving 25 percent or more of his income, and is only in it to sell you some life insurance?

Do your own taxes, and then get an accountant to confirm that your work is accurate. In fact, only do that if you have some complicated holdings that need the extra eye. It's an indication of helplessness to go to an accountant during the period where more than 95 percent of your income is from a W2 job. Even when your holdings become complex, educate yourself to the point where you may knowledgeably seek specialized help from an accountant that fits the bill.

If you are reliant on people with titles, degrees, and certifications to handle the basic stuff ordinary people deal with all the time you're helpless. You're throwing away money on problems that can be researched in just a few hours of applied effort. Hire a specialist only in select and truly unique situations, or after you've done exhaustive research and know exactly what you need done, and how you want it done.

Now the folks who play in the big leagues with money will argue the opposite. They will argue it's not worth your time to learn about these things, and that it's better to hire a specialist. And, their advice is correct—but only for them. Those earning hundreds of thousands of dollars per year absolutely should hire out as much as they can, focusing their time and energy on activities that produce such large income! Those earning $500,000+ per year are silly to patch their own drywall, or fix a toilet. But, Average Joe earning $50,000 per year had better believe that fixing his own toilet is going to have a significant impact on his finances. It's highly likely he will have to pay someone else far more than $25 per hour (about his hourly rate). For example, a plumber will typically charge $75 to $150 per hour for his services. If Joe opts not to hire out a plumbing job and does the work himself, he effectively pays himself $75 to $150 per hour, tax-free.

This is not to say that professionals don't have their place. This is to point out that too many Americans are too soft, weak, and scared to handle ordinary affairs on their own because the professionals in industries like law, accounting, medicine, financial services, home services, and the like sound gloom and doom when folks attempt to tackle even the basics of their profession. Trust me, if you are truly motivated to learn about what you need to do, you can tackle many of the routine things that other people hand over to specialists. Most of the time, the consequences won't be memorable. So what if you screw up the plumbing and it leaks all over your floor? Shut the water off and *then* call the plumber. Sure, you're out on that one project, but you've learned something. Work hard to become increasingly independent of specialists. For the rest of your life, you will hear lawyers, accountants, doctors, financial planners, and the like telling you how to run your life and telling you that you ought not to do things yourself. Forget them. Do it yourself.

If you take the position that you're responsible for all of the outcomes in your life, you will find the cost savings to be in the tens of thousands or hundreds of thousands of dollars over the next decade or so. Yes, you will make mistakes, and yes, you should consult with these professionals from time to time. But, only after you have a reasonable understanding of what it is you are trying to do, and what success looks like.

Getting by on Less than "the Best"

Here in America, people tend to have this complex whereby they want "the best" and are constantly seeking out "the best." Those who take a position in which they will not settle for anything less than the best (when it comes to consumption, at least) are robbing themselves of valuable years of their lives. "The best" is ridiculously expensive and quite often, imperceptibly better than "quite good."

"The best" wine might cost hundreds or thousands of dollars a bottle, whereas cheap wine might be $8 a bottle. Who's happier at the end of the bottle? A 40" HD TV might cost $250. The same TV in 4K Ultra HD might be $2500. Even if the picture is marginally clearer, is the experience ten times greater watching a 4K Ultra HD TV than a regular HD TV? This logic applies to almost every consumption choice available. Doctors, lawyers, accountants, psychiatrists, computers, smartphones, cars, clothing, jewelry, gyms, first class vs. economy, seats at the ball game, and more all have low and high cost options.

A great example is in school selection. Parents will pay incredible costs to ensure their children can go to the best schools. They will buy housing they can't afford, commute absurd distances throughout the day, and work jobs with a soul-crushing lack of opportunity or creativity, just to rest their heads at night in "the best" school district.

The motivation behind this decision is admirable. But, it's likely many fail to think through the implications of this decision, and how it might impact their family life. Did they consider the possibility that a long commute might result in a lack of time hanging out with the kids at home (a critical factor in children's long-term development)? Did they consider the possibility that taking on such a large mortgage payment might inhibit their ability to send their children to college? Did they consider the possibility their child might pursue a high paying trade, like computer science, welding, electrical work, or another trade skill that won't require an education from "the best" schools? Did they consider that living frugally and using the surplus cash generated to invest in startup businesses, real estate, or other investments might be a great way to teach their children life skills that even "the best" schools can't teach? Did they consider that they are giving up the opportunity to have any other lifestyle than their current one, simply so that their kids can go to "the best" school in the short-term?

Do they really need the best schools? Might more time at home, and early financial freedom be more than enough to compensate for moving into the second, or even third best school district in the area? Might the benefits of early financial freedom and the opportunities it provides for more parenting time and flexibility outweigh the disadvantages of choosing a school district that's more affordable? Are the "average" schools in the area really so terrible that they simply can't bear to send their kids there even when that decision comes with enormous advantages in almost every other area of their lives, financially and otherwise?

The point isn't to buy things that are low quality. The point is to understand that every day we have to make choices. And frequently, you'll find excellence (rather than "the best"), is quite good enough.

Slowly and Steadily Chip Away

For some reason, people tend to think they can start saving more money and become a frugal superhero overnight. This is just not the case. Deliberately and significantly altering a lifestyle is a time-consuming, intentional process. Changing a mindset from "I have to call a professional" to "I can easily do this myself" is something that will take months or years. It doesn't happen overnight. It might take six months to find a suitable new place to live. It might take several weeks or months to successfully transition from daily lunches out to regularly preparing delicious food you actually enjoy eating.

Designing a low cost lifestyle is just as difficult and requires just as much time, effort, and planning to optimize as does investing, scaling your income, or building businesses. It just happens to have a huge financial impact on those seeking early financial freedom from a starting point involving little to no assets and a moderate income.

Conclusion

The wealth building process begins with a close examination of one's expenses and thought process when it comes to spending money. By embracing frugality and doing whatever is in your power to protect your hard-earned dollars, you will begin to set the wheels of the wealth-building process in motion.

No, you do not need to buy the best—you can get by just as happily with acceptable goods and services. Do not fall victim to marketing messages of those telling you that you deserve the best. You don't deserve the best. You deserve freedom. You deserve power over your day. Buy that, instead of something that's overpriced and under delivers.

No, you do not need to call a professional to solve your problems. You are quite capable of handling life and dealing with everyday problems on your own. You're trying to become wealthy at an early age right? Well, act like an adult. Fix your own sink, change your own oil, and learn to spot competence—and to fire incompetence.

This is not about being cheap. It is about wanting early financial freedom so badly that the choice not to spend is an easy one. Take pride in the fact that you live efficiently and don't blow your money on outlandish toys that destroy wealth. Far from being something to aspire to, ostentatious displays of wealth should *offend* your sensibilities as they so obviously delay financial freedom for a short-lived material pleasure. The guy at the stoplight with the shiny new jacked-up pickup truck should look like a fool to you, not as someone to be admired and emulated.

Remember that every dollar you spend is after-tax, and every dollar you earn is pre-tax. Thus, it's inefficient to earn a dollar, when there are equal or greater dollars begging to be rescued. Remember that those starting out on the wealth building journey will impact their personal lives far less by cutting out the waste than they will by using their free time to try to start businesses or work second jobs. And remember why you're saving in the first place. You are saving so you can buy your freedom.

Yes, this book will discuss increasing income and producing excellent investment returns as part of hastening early financial freedom. Frugality and lifestyle design shouldn't come at the expense of income production, and do not worry that you will need to save your way through to hundreds of thousands or even millions in net worth. However, as a first step, most Americans earning median incomes will find that serious progress is made at first through the intelligent and intentional application of frugal living and preservation of earned income.

Contrast that with the decision to move from a fancy apartment that costs $1300 per month to moving to a smaller two-bedroom apartment with a roommate for the same price. This decision saves $650 per month ($7800 per year) and does not involve sacrificing any day-to-day recreational activities.

Tackling small variable expenses such as forgoing your lattes from Starbucks in the morning, your nightlife, and your happy hour with friends and colleagues will require willpower. It will require you to the form good habits, and apply long-term emotional thinking each and every time you prepare to purchase something. You will need to decide on a case-by-case basis whether an expense is worthwhile, and when it is isn't. Relying on willpower alone is not enough—and it is unnecessary given that the variable expense categories are relatively small for Average Joe. *Variable expenses aren't the problem.* And, they can be the toughest expenses to truly cut out. Instead, if you focus on the large fixed parts of your budget, you can feel free to spend on small luxuries with no regrets. Understand that $50 a week on small meals or treats with friends and family will not materially impact your financial freedom, and doesn't need to be sacrificed.

Of course, if you are spending thousands of dollars per month on unnecessary shopping, meals out, or other entertainment, you have an obvious spending problem that needs to be addressed. You'll need to figure that one out on your own, as this book assumes that attaining early financial freedom is more of a priority for you than that type of spending. But, there's no need to eradicate the small pleasures in life that you truly enjoy on a day-to-day basis if you are willing to do the big things right instead.

Don't sacrifice the little things. Change the big things.

Let's start with the obvious and tackle our housing expense first.

Renting Discussion

The best way to eliminate housing expenses will be through a special type of purchase that will be discussed in chapter 4. However, most folks that are working to accumulate their first $25,000 in assets will be renting in the meantime.

The typical wage-earner, without access to free or exceptionally low-cost housing, will be left a rather obvious choice: *Find an apartment that can be affordably rented, make sure it's as close to work as practical, and try to split the costs with a roommate or two.* That's it.

Let's consider an example. Andrew and James began their careers making exactly the same amount of money. James chose to live in the fanciest part of Denver close to the bars and city nightlife. Andrew lived with a roommate in a cheap apartment close to work. Andrew's rent was $550 per month. James's was $1200. They lived just six miles apart. A year later, Andrew's housing decision, combined with the other positive lifestyle choices it encouraged, enabled him to accumulate and save $7800 in rent, $2000 in commuting costs, and $1500 in entertainment expenses, all after tax, relative to James.

This scenario is repeated in major cities all over the country. The cost of living in the best part of town is extremely expensive. Living just a few miles away can be much less expensive. Still want to enjoy things in the best part of town? Spend a portion of the difference in rent driving or taking an Uber to that part of town and pocket the net. The same goes for living alone. Single individuals pursuing early financial freedom should understand that living alone costs nearly double what it costs to split an apartment a few ways by sharing the space and cost with a roommate. Families pursuing early financial freedom will, of course, make up for the inability to split housing costs by having two income earners.

Living in a cheap apartment convenient to the workplace is the single most important thing you can do to start saving money. No other single change will have a bigger impact on your spending, as a typical American, than where you choose to rest your head at night. If you are interested in financial freedom and are unable/unwilling to buy a residence that will improve your financial position, rent a low-cost apartment with some roommates in an area that is close to work. Do this for a year or two until you're in a personal financial position that's conducive to successfully buying a first property. How to purchase a first property will be covered in depth in chapter 5.

Your Commute

After housing, the largest fixed expense in Average Joe's life is that of his commute. The American commute is an incredible expense that destroys billions of dollars in wealth, hurts the planet, and leaves good people with, literally, years of life spent risking their lives daily behind the wheel.

In spite of his bitter resistance to this claim, Joe's commuting costs are *not* fixed. The fact he spends almost an hour of his day in the car going to and from work is a personal choice he made, a decision which is repeated part of life" in *any* part of the country. It can always be changed. Always. Every single person who has a long commute has made the combinatorial choice to live where they live and work where they work. It is a personal choice made at the individual level, and the *decision* to buy or rent a home and take a job in locations that are far apart from one another keeps middle class Americans middle class and Average Joe average. Millions of people commute out of cities with excellent jobs to work an average job in a city that is some distance away, even as others commute into *their* town for high paying work. They think their jobs or their homes are special. They are not. This applies to everyone. Too often, Average Joe dismisses his commute as a part of life, as a fixed expense that cannot be changed in his circumstance.

Shortening your commute can make you happier, healthier, and wealthier. It can speed you down the path toward early financial freedom. Don't be Average Joe. Move your home closer to your work, or if that truly is infeasible, move your work closer to your home by finding new work.

Food

Food makes up about 12.5 percent or one-eighth of Average Joe's budget and is the third largest line item in his spending pie chart. The great news is that much of this spending ($3000 of $7000) comes from eating food away from home—fast food, restaurants, bars, etc., and can be readily reduced with immediate benefits to his health, wealth, and happiness.

Joe tends to eat out at expensive, unhealthy restaurants; the result is he's broke and fat. Amazingly, it's well within Joe's power to eliminate much of his eating out budget and instead feed himself delicious, self-prepared food for less than $300 per month per person.

The secret Joe missed is that he needs to prepare most of his food, most of the time, with healthy purchases from reasonable (that means: not Whole Foods) grocery stores. If he does this, he can immediately reduce his spending to less than half that of the Average American. This does not mean Joe has to eliminate his spending on meals out entirely. He does not have to miss lunch with the boss or his colleagues, or skip happy hour with his friends. No, all Joe has to do is follow the tips below:

- Always have the ready option for a delicious and healthy meal

- Forgo truly unhealthy and horrible fast food entirely

- Enjoy meals out with friends and family when opportunity arises and makes sense

- Never go out to eat because he doesn't have anything prepared
- Always be prepared with healthy snacks like fruits, nuts, and vegetables

Healthy nuts, berries, fruits, lean meats, fish, and healthy grains are not what's killing Joe's budget. Yes, healthy food is more expensive than, say, ramen. But, it's absurd to eat unhealthy food in the name of saving money. Joe should eat wholesome food every day. He just needs to make his default option a healthy choice from a grocery store.

This alone can make you happier, healthier, more productive, and of course, wealthier. If you have a large box or bag of healthy nuts at your desk or in your lunch box at work, and the next best option is chips or candy from the vending machine, you are highly likely to snack on what's within reach. If you don't have snacks, then your dollars will flow into the vending machine, and fat will flow to your stomach. Nobody gets fat or goes broke snacking on almonds and apples, but plenty of people empty their pockets and line their stomachs with soda and candy from vending machines.

A healthy diet will help you avoid health problems and keep you focused. And, healthy food should not break your budget. Be reasonable, and be healthy with your eating.

Personal Insurance and Pensions

The primary purpose of insurance should be to eliminate distractions from your other life and financial pursuits. Proper insurance should allow you to go about your day without making decisions based on fear. You shouldn't be afraid to drive around and get in an accident, or have a sickness unduly devastate your life. You also shouldn't fear for your family, heirs, or the affairs of others if you pass away. Insurance is a personal decision, and the amount and type of coverage is something best left to self-education followed by the help of a great insurance agent.

Typically, the best way to reduce insurance premiums is to increase deductibles. Average Joe lives basically paycheck to paycheck, and even a $3000 expense is an emergency he can't handle. Those aspiring to financial freedom will quickly save $5000, $10,000 or more, and manage their money and investments such that they have ready access to funds. Therefore, a $3000 deductible is no big deal.

Make sure your insurance protects you from major problems that might otherwise financially ruin you. But, think twice before buying insurance

Chapter 3
What to Do with Money as You Save It

Chapters 1 and 2 should have helped you understand the theory behind frugality and develop a practical plan to live on less than half your take-home pay; all in the context of building up your first $25,000. After reading those two chapters, you should understand what you need to do to put yourself in position to save thousands of dollars per month on a middle class income. Now, it's time to deploy those savings in such a way as to develop your first year of financial runway. Your goal is stockpile a reserve capable of funding your frugal lifestyle for around a full year.

Unlike many Americans who struggle to make ends meet, you now face a new problem. A good problem. You now have to decide how to deploy your rapidly expanding savings so that they extend your financial runway as much as possible. There are three initial steps that should be completed, in order, for the seeker of early financial freedom to build up that one-year stockpile. These three steps are (1) to build up an emergency fund of $1000 to $2000; (2) to pay off all "bad debts" (we define this term below) and build strong credit; and then (3) to build up one year of financial runway in the form of cash or equivalents

By completing these three steps, readers will set themselves up for the next phase of wealth generation, discussed in part II. They will have the cash and credit they need to buy a home with ease, and will have the financial runway they need to pursue career opportunities with little risk of financial ruin.

Central to the discussion in this chapter will be the concepts of debt—both good and bad debt—and credit. We must pay off our bad debts immediately, and treat them as a financial crisis. Good debts can still delay financial freedom, but may not need to be paid off early if money can be put to higher and better use in the meantime. While paying off bad debts and managing other debts, readers will want to focus on improving their credit scores as much as possible, and increase their access to credit.

"Bad" Debt vs. "Good" Debt

Bad Debts

Bad debts include debts financed at high (10 percent or more) interest rates, that incur late fees, or that impact your credit score. These types of debts are actively draining your wallet and preventing you from reaping the advantages of a strong credit score. These debts are an emergency, and you should not focus on building wealth beyond a small emergency reserve prior to eliminating bad debts from your life. Save up just enough cash to make sure you don't take on an additional bad debt due to bad luck, and then begin paying down your bad debts as aggressively as you can.

Some examples of bad debts include:
- Credit card debt (often charge high interest)
- Fines and parking tickets (often incur late fees)
- Any delinquent or high interest consumer debts
- Payday loans (ugh)

These types of debts are actively killing your financial position and damaging your credit. It's likely that if you have these kinds of debts and haven't taken action to begin paying them off promptly, you have collections agencies after you. This is where finances begin to spiral out of control for many people as their debt coverage and the fees accompanying their debt consumes their disposable income, and creates new and larger amounts of debt.

If you have bad debt, don't buy luxuries. Don't go out for dinner. Instead, stop wasting money and pay off those debts as quickly as possible. It's foolish and dangerous to pursue investments, consider buying property, or otherwise make large financial decisions with bad debts looming overhead.

There are several schools of thought for how to pay down bad debts. Two excellent ones are as follows:
- Method 1: The Debt Snowball. Championed by personal finance and anti-debt guru Dave Ramsey, this concept involves paying

off the smallest debt first, then moving to the next smallest, and proceeding so on and so forth. The advantage to this method is it offers the debtor the chance to score some easy wins with smaller debts to get them in the mindset and habit of paying down their debt completely. The disadvantage is it's not technically the most efficient way to pay down debt. It's a more efficient utilization of your money to pay down debts via the second method.

- Method 2: Pay the highest interest rate debt first. This is a more efficient method than the Debt Snowball approach because it involves paying down the most expensive debt first, and will result in a more efficient deployment of savings. The downside is that those with large high-interest debt may find themselves paying their debt for months or years before eliminating any single debt from their records.

Assume an individual has the following debts:

- A $5000 debt at 10 percent interest
- A $1000 debt at 8 percent interest
- A $500 debt at 6 percent interest

Under the debt snowball approach, the $500 debt would be tackled first, then the $1000 debt, then the $5000 debt. The individual would have the satisfaction of eliminating two of the three debts rapidly, and use that confidence to tackle the third debt. On the other hand, paying the $5000 debt down first might result in less total interest paid, and would likely allow the debtor to pay down his total debt a little faster.

Two Quick Notes on Paying Down Debt

Note 1: Try negotiation. Hospital debt, credit card debt, or other similar high-interest debt, can often be negotiated. This is especially true of delinquent debt that's several years old. It's amazing to watch folks with delinquent five-figure hospital debt negotiate their way down to just a few thousand or even a few hundred dollars with a single phone call. If you decide to negotiate your debt down, here are some tips for when you call your creditor:

- Understand that many delinquent debts are *never* paid, so the collector wins when you agree to pay even a fraction of the total amount owed.

- Keep in mind that a long call might be necessary—but even two straight hours is worth it if you can negotiate the bill down by hundreds or thousands of dollars.

- Be polite, but make it clear you're willing to take as long as it takes on the phone to bring down your debt amount.

- Your creditor has every right to refuse to reduce what you owe, so don't count on getting it lowered.

Note 2: Self-Educate. The second note is that if you have many years of old bad debts (old in this case meaning more than three to four years old), you'll probably want to do more research and talk to some professional folks about tackling it in the best way. This is a situation where intelligent self-study can reap large rewards. Did you know that making payments on a debt that's really old (several years delinquent) can actually have negative impacts on your financial position, and in some cases, you may not need to pay off a debt that is more than seven to ten years in default? There's quite a bit of nuance on this subject, so if you're looking to begin paying down debts and have a long track record of bed debt, do your homework.

Good Debts

In addition to bad debts, there are so called "good" debts. These debts can include things like:

- Home mortgages

- Student loans

- Car loans

- Personal loans

- Any other debt that is current and financed at low interest rates

These debts are commonly referred to as "good" debts, but that's a fallacy. These debts can accrue into the tens of thousands of dollars or even into the hundreds of thousands of dollars. While they may not be actively damaging your credit score, or bearing unreasonably high interest, they are to be avoided, just like bad debts. If you aspire to early financial freedom, you will not accrue the debt needlessly.

There are two ways to deal with a large amount of low-interest "good" debt. First, suck it up and pay it off—with the exception of home mortgage debt. It's a huge advantage to have little to no debt when attempting to scale toward early financial freedom. Understand that the debt will slow you down, and that it will take you years longer than the next guy—without debt—to begin working aggressively toward early financial freedom.

The second option is to make the minimum payments on the debt, and build up your year of financial runway even with that debt. True, you will have to make payments on the debt, which will increase your monthly expenses and thus increase the amount of money needed to cover one year of expenses. But, by building up a reserve of at least one year's annual spending, you will give yourself the same flexibility as the guy without debt.

While the best way to hasten along the path to early financial freedom is to avoid these debts entirely, many readers will be starting from a position in which they have already accumulated a large amount of personal debt. If that's the case, then note that it's unnecessary to entirely pay down your debt before progressing with the next steps in this book. As long as the debt is financed at a low interest rate (probably less than 5 to 6 percent), you can make the minimum payments on the debt, and begin accumulating cash outside of it. For example, there is little advantage to paying down a car loan with 2 percent interest early. But, it might make a lot of sense to pay down or refinance a student loan charging 7 or 8 percent interest. In between, the choice will come down to personal preference.

Credit

Credit has been mentioned several times, and for good reason. One's credit score and access to credit can play a huge role in determining their exposure to financial opportunities and in helping them build a longer financial runway faster. When it comes to credit, most people fall into two camps: those with acceptable credit and those with poor credit.

Those aspiring to early financial freedom will want to achieve two things as they pertain to credit here in part I to give themselves the strongest position from which to move forward. First, they will want to improve their credit score as much as possible. Second, they will want to put themselves in a position with as much access to credit as possible.

Improving and Maintaining Credit

Credit scores have a surprisingly large impact on American life. Those with poor scores find themselves denied housing opportunities, car loans, credit cards, and even jobs. In a very real sense, this score affects where you live, how you get around, how you buy stuff, and your career opportunities. Those with good scores find those types of basic choices to be straightforward and simple, while those with poor scores struggle daily.

A credit score is a reflection of one's financial dignity. Specifically, it is a reflection of one's ability to handle debts. Late and missed payments hurt scores, while on-time payments and debt reduction can increase scores.

Improving one's credit score is simple and straightforward. The first step is to go check your credit score by getting a free copy of your report from one of the three major credit bureaus (TransUnion, Equifax, and Experian), or by accessing the information through a third-party website like Credit Karma. Check all the accounts and look for any potential errors—they happen all the time, and need to be resolved so that you can improve your score. Look at the factors that make up a credit score, their relative weight, and how you score in each category.

The second step is to simply get current on your debts and begin making your payments on time. Look at your debts and set up automatic payments for them. In some cases, you might have to call the person holding your debt to find out how to begin making payments on it.

The third step is to begin aggressively paying down your debt. The less you owe, the more your score will improve. After getting current on your debts, start paying down the highest interest debt first while making the minimum payments on the rest or employ the Debt Snowball approach and pay down the debt with the smallest balance first.

To maintain good credit, pay your bills on time, and don't take on more debt than you can easily repay. Ever.

Increasing Access to Credit

Increasing access to credit can provide lots of flexibility for those seeking early financial freedom. More credit is better than less credit in most cases. Suppose that John has one credit card with a limit of $5000. If John is able to increase his limit to $10,000 over a year or two, he reaps many advantages with few disadvantages.

As John is pursuing early financial freedom, he will not be purchasing more luxuries with his larger credit balance, but his credit increase can be used in a pinch, if necessary. Furthermore, credit scores are impacted by credit utilization. If John usually spends about $2000 per month, all on his credit card, then his credit utilization is 40 percent on a credit limit of

$5000. If his utilization drops to 20 percent on a credit limit of $10,000, then his credit score—which is based in part on credit utilization rate—will improve as a result.

Individuals who are unable to control their credit card spending will obviously not want access to more credit, but this book is not for those folks. If you are a disciplined spender who will never abuse a large credit limit, and have just a few credit cards, it can make sense to request a credit increase every six months. This can be done by calling your credit card company or visiting their website. Ask if your request will result in a hard inquiry on your credit report, which can temporarily reduce your score and remain on your credit report for two years. Understand whether that tradeoff is to your advantage.

The First Three Milestones in the Journey to Financial Freedom

Okay, so at this point you are saving up thousands of dollars per month due to your efficient lifestyle and have a general understanding of good and bad debt. You also know how to go about improving your credit score and increasing your access to credit. It's time to take that cash and knowledge and apply it directly to your financial position. There are three simple steps to follow when building out the first year of financial runway:

1. Build $1000 to $2000 in emergency funds immediately.

2. Start paying off bad debts and get back to zero.

3. Build up about $25,000 in working capital.

Once you've accomplished these three milestones, you will have the opportunity to pursue a more scalable career, house hack, or even take a six-month to one year shot at starting a business full-time. If you're not interested in making those changes, then excess cash will be used to acquire income-producing assets until early financial freedom is achieved.

Step #1: Emergency Funds

"But this isn't investing!" says the ambitious, raring-to-go twenty-something who's living paycheck to paycheck and playing around with her $2000 in stocks.

Building an emergency fund is perhaps the *single best investment* available. The first $1000 to $2000 in the bank results in a state of mind unavailable to the guy who has bad debt and lacks emergency funds. The person with a small cash cushion gets to sleep at night, knowing they can afford next month's rent and their next meal. This ensures food, rent, and basic transportation are accessible, and $1000 to $2000 in the bank can bail out the guy with small problems.

> *Meet Bobby. Bobby is twenty-five and living for the first time on his own. He has a ton of bad debt, and never has any money in his bank account. He doesn't really think about money much, and spends his whole paycheck on nights out with friends, movie tickets, and whenever he has extra cash, a fancy trip. The problem? He's constantly asking his parents for money and financial favors. His father co-signed his apartment lease because Bobby's credit was too poor. Bobby regularly turns to his parents for help with the basics of life, including the Internet bill, rent, his car payment, and his phone bill.*
>
> *The cost of this economic aid is that Bobby's parents have a lot of say in his life, relative to his friends. They visit him frequently, and expect him to attend dinner with them several times per week. They expect his place to be furnished and decorated to their standard, and disapprove of the beer in his fridge and the personal effects that he collects. Bobby is constantly uncomfortable in his apartment and knows that Mom and Dad feel perfectly at ease arriving on short notice. This is a hefty price to pay due to a lack of financial control. If Bobby were able to build an emergency fund and maintain a strong savings rate, Mom and Dad lose economic control over his life and Bobby gets to live life on his terms, not those of his parents. Were that need for financial aid to disappear, Bobby might have a stronger, more equal relationship with his parents and command more respect from his friends. Therefore, Bobby's goal is to move toward a more independent financial position.*

The first step in this journey is the accumulation of $1000 to $2000 in savings. Bobby will be able to avoid most of the small embarrassing requests for money with this initial reserve, and will avoid incurring new bad debts without having to go to Mom and Dad for aid or increasing his already high credit card balance.

The first $1000 to $2000 in savings provides the financial peace of mind and cushion to avoid the daily expenses and mental discomfort that go along with being broke. However, $1000 to $2000 is a general range and the size of an emergency fund is specific to the individual. While $1000 to $2000 in cash won't prevent large problems from causing financial distress, it should be enough to cover the majority of small problems in day-to-day life, and allows one the ability to move to step two.

Step #2: Paying Down Debts and Improving Credit Scores

As long as you have bad debts, there is no point in building an emergency fund beyond $1000 to $2000. The entire point of the emergency fund in step one is to avoid creating new bad debt and to preserve financial dignity when encountering life's petty problems. Think about it: if you need to get the tires replaced on your car and can't pay for it, you'll incur a bad debt. If you can't pay a speeding ticket, you accumulate bad debt and a hefty late fee. No emergencies.

Once Bobby is able to cover his day-to-day expenses and accrue this emergency fund, he can deploy his savings toward paying down high interest credit card debt and getting current on his other debts. In doing this, he'll be on his way to becoming debt free with rapidly improving credit. He'll be able to move into a new apartment rented without any assistance from Mom and Dad and begin living life on his terms, as an independent adult. No longer will he be a dependent.

Step #3: Build a Reserve of $10,000 to $25,000

Assuming you've no bad debts, it's time to build up the first $10,000 to $25,000 in wealth. Don't cheat when accumulating this wealth. Home equity, retirement account contributions, the value of your car, and the value of other items you don't intend to sell *don't count*. This first $10,000 to $25,000 in wealth needs to be accessible, available, and you must be willing to use it to advance your financial position.

Assuming Bobby earns a median salary and lives frugally, he should be able to save at a minimum $1500 per month after tax, in cash. At this savings rate, accessible wealth between $10,000 and $25,000 can be built in about a year of hard work. This is tough. This is the part of the process that can feel like a grind. But it is incredibly important. It is the foundation of the rest of this book, and the turning point at which one is presented with options to make more dramatic changes. Bobby will go from merely self-sufficient to prosperous during this time period. While the process will be month to month and occasionally feel painfully slow, Bobby will emerge after twelve to eighteen months in an extremely advantageous position with his first year of financial runway built out.

The person with a year of financial runway on modest salary gives himself the option to do one or several of these things:

- Place a down payment on a first property
- Pursue a new career opportunity without fear of running out of cash
- Acquire a meaningful asset
- Attempt to build a business or income stream full-time for up to twelve months

Understand that these options are available to the individual who has accumulated $10,000 to $25,000 in readily accessible wealth *only* if that individual has a frugal lifestyle. Twenty-five thousand dollars will fund a lifestyle that costs $2000 per month for over a year, if necessary. One who spends $4000 per month will need to accumulate significantly more cash in order to expose themselves to the advantages listed above. This is why the book begins with a discussion of frugality and lifestyle design. A frugal lifestyle enables faster accumulation of assets for a middle-class wage earner *and* reduces the amount of wealth needed to develop a lengthy financial runway.

The first year of financial runway purchases access to opportunity. Giving yourself the ability to pursue new careers and higher income is the best purchase you can possibly make on the path to early financial freedom. The other great news is that this money doesn't have to be stored in your bank account. The money can actually be stored in things like after-tax brokerage accounts. You can purchase stocks, bonds, funds, and other publicly-traded securities as you approach and surpass the first $10,000 to $25,000 in accessible wealth. These types of investments often generate returns far in excess of the paltry interest paid by savings accounts.

Some folks believe that keeping their working capital account in stocks is too risky, and that's a completely valid argument. It is up to you to decide. Would you rather have a large cash reserve available and kept safe in a bank account? Or, would you rather keep that money invested, knowing that those investments might lose value, and that you may have to add money to the reserve from time to time to make up for those occasional losses? It's up to you decide whether you are okay with placing your initial savings at risk in exchange for the possibility of returns. We talk more about what to do with this funding later in the book in chapter 9.

An Example of How to Think through Debt Decisions Correctly

Meet Greg. Greg is thirty-one, lives in Orange County in Southern California and works at night earning tips. He spends a lot of time during the day learning about investing. He's fortunate to have health insurance and a 401(k) as a restaurant server. Greg has about $10,000 of debt, and $5000 of it is high-interest debt. This is in the form of a large credit balance, and a judgment. The other $5000 is in the form of a low-interest student loan. Greg always pays himself first by saving 30 percent of his income and puts 50 percent of that income toward the debt. Greg's income is roughly $1000 per week, mostly in tips from his job as a restaurant server. He's been working hard on his credit score and went from a 495 to a 650 between January and June by getting current on his bad debts. Greg has a few assets, which include $3000 in stocks and $2000 in cash savings). Greg's goal is to live for free by buying a duplex within thirty miles from work using an FHA owner-occupied loan with a down payment out of savings, then renting out one of the units of the duplex while living in the other with a roommate. As Greg saves a ton of money already, he was also going to Uber on the side and look into starting a property management company with his free time if he can find business.

Greg's question: *Should I focus on paying down all my debt (good and bad) first, or instead build up my first year of financial runway?*

Greg is a guy who has really begun getting his act together. He clearly has a troubled financial past involving credit card debt, tax liens, and even a judgment, but he recognized this and began taking serious action toward improving his position. Amazingly, he increased his credit score from a dismal 495 to a 650 in less than six months! This is actually not uncommon. He's also managed to acquire some assets—$5000 combined between his stock account and his savings account. He has done all of this while making less than $50,000 per year as a server.

The core fundamentals of what he is doing are 100 percent correct, and he is applying the basics of living frugally, earning extra income, and investing the difference. He is on his way toward early financial freedom, assuming he remains consistent. If Greg wanted to move toward his goal of buying a duplex and living for free, he would be wise to pay off only his bad debts, the ones that are over 6 to 7 percent or so and the ones that are affecting his credit. Then, he should focus on building up his savings so that he can make the down payment on a duplex. His low interest debt, so long as he is current, will not materially detract from his ability to buy a property. If Greg can wipe out his housing expense by turning his home into an income-producing asset, where rent from his roommates and tenants covers his mortgage payment, then he is wise to pursue this strategy before paying down low-interest debt that's not affecting his credit score.

Conclusion

Those working full-time jobs wishing to pursue early financial freedom will find saving the first $10,000 to $25,000 to be the hardest part. It takes sacrifice, perseverance, thought, energy, and most of all, time. There are no cheat codes. *Only* cash or equivalents count. Only wealth that you are willing to deploy in pursuit of your goals counts. Focus on building wealth that will put you in a position where you can take advantage of opportunity and rapidly build the financial runway that will lead you to early financial freedom.

Side jobs, side hustles, freelance work, and weekend work may expedite this accumulation phase. But, the real determinant of how long this will take is your spending. Cut back on *everything* that doesn't bring you happiness. Don't forget to enjoy life, but understand that wasteful spending can eliminate hours or weeks of hard work. Save your way to your first real opportunities. Save to the point where you can survive for a full year without the need for wage-paying work.

Once achieved, you will have completely eliminated bad debt from your life, you will have the freedom and flexibility to remove yourself from an intolerable work environment with a year long financial runway, and you are well prepared to begin thinking about how to make the next large leap forward in the pursuit of financial freedom.

Part II
From $25,000 to $100,000 through Housing and Income Generation

Congratulations! Getting from zero or negative net worth to tens of thousands of dollars in cash and a yearlong financial runway is a remarkable accomplishment that few achieve at an early age. You did it in just over a year by living frugally and putting a priority on saving up your funds. Very impressive. Now it's time to make the next leap forward. Now it's time to understand the factors that will actually make a difference as you try to go from $25,000 to $100,000 in net worth. It's time to extend your financial runway to three, five, or even ten years. It's time to take bold actions—ones that set you apart. It's time to get rich.

Of course, it's possible to save your way to wealth by investing consistently. Yes, you can earn a modest salary, save and invest your savings in assets that produce an average return, and slowly inch toward financial freedom. An aggressive saver at a median income might be able to go from a standing start with little to no assets to financial freedom in ten to fifteen years through hardcore savings alone. But that's too slow. At best, you might accumulate $500,000 in wealth (perhaps the minimum amount needed to sustain modest early financial freedom) in a little over a decade. But, you can do better. Much better. You can accelerate that outcome by many years if you focus on things that have the ability to scale.

In this part of the book, you will learn how to transform your housing from a monthly liability into an asset. And, you will learn what you need to do to double or even triple your income. You will learn how to put yourself in a position where generating $75,000 per year in *wealth* is achievable.

Why go through that first section at all, if this is the part that has the opportunity to scale? Well, the reason is that you *now have $25,000* (or a

51

year of financial runway) to deploy toward scalable activities. That $25,000 is what you will use to turn your home into an income-producing asset. That $25,000 is what you will use to buy your way into a scalable income. Read on to find out how.

Chapter 4
Turning Your Largest Expense into an Income Producing Asset

In chapter 2, we met Average Joe. We analyzed his spending and concluded housing was his largest expense. In that chapter, the only suggestion we could give Average Joe was to move into a cheaper apartment and share it with a roommate. Poor Joe. The advice is valid, but only applied to his circumstances because he didn't have the resources to actually make a big decision that would entirely wipe out his housing expenses.

Not anymore. Part I showed Average Joe how to go about accumulating his first $25,000 in wealth, in readily accessible cash or cash equivalents that he'd be willing to spend. Joe's savings habit, conscientious debt reduction, and consistency over the past twelve to eighteen months have resulted in a situation where he has readily accessible wealth, a strong savings rate, and excellent credit. Now Joe can move out of his cramped two-person apartment. Now Joe can buy a property.

Average Joe's Housing Dilemma

Let's reintroduce Average Joe. Average Joe is a typical guy earning $50,000 per year and now has plentiful savings as a result of employing the strategies in part I. Joe has also recently begun to carefully analyze his personal finances and has wisely decided to look into building wealth by tackling his largest single expense: his housing. Joe isn't a fan of seeing almost a third of his income go toward his rent, and he wants to reduce that expense.

Average Joe has already decided where he wants to live; he's a young professional and wants to live near the nice part of town so he can be near all the fun things his city offers, his work, and of course, good schools for any future children. Within his target living area, he spots an opportunity. A duplex has come on the market, and remarkably, it's available to either purchase or rent.

Joe happens to work for a well-known company where he projects costs and expenses by building spreadsheets. Joe wisely decides to do what no one else in the working world ever seems to do and creates a spreadsheet analyzing the cost of his own housing expenses. Crazy, huh?

Joe's Financial Model

Joe maps out the financial impact three different ways; three cases (get it? Like a *case study*?) in which he could live in his favorite part of town and in this duplex. In the process of doing so, Joe realizes this study is applicable to almost anyone deciding whether to rent, buy, or "house hack" (buy, then rent out part of the house to others). Joe does his best to think through all the costs, rents, and other financial factors that might come into play under each scenario. His goal is to see how he can live for the lowest cost, but still reside in his favorite part of town.

Joe thoughtfully builds the spreadsheet in a way that others can easily follow.[1] In fact, he even highlights in bright yellow all the assumptions he made specific to this property that he was considering, so that anyone else who downloaded the spreadsheet could change those inputs and see if his conclusions have any relevance to their own situations.

No, people looking at this spreadsheet don't need to be Microsoft Excel wizards like Joe to play around with the numbers, so long as they only change the numbers highlighted in yellow!

With that, let's talk about the conclusions from this case study, and Joe's three choices.

Case #1: Joe Rents Half of the Duplex as a Tenant

Joe is currently a renter, so this is no big change for him, just a little bit of an upgrade in location.

Joe's renting assumptions:

- The property is listed at $300,000.
- Monthly rents are 1 percent of the list price.
- Joe pays 0.5 percent of the purchase price in rent per month

[1] See them at https://www.biggerpockets.com/files/user/ScottTrench/file/house-hack-vs-buy-sfr-vs-rent.

($1500 per month) because he only lives in one of the two units.

- Rents increase over time with inflation at 3.4 percent.

In this case, the monthly rents for Joe come to $1500 per month, or $18,000 per year in the first year. Joe will build no wealth through this process and the cost of living is very easy to calculate over time, as rents increase with inflation. Joe notes that if he pursues this strategy, he doesn't have to bring "money down" like he would in a home purchase, and he can immediately put that money in the stock market or spend it as he wishes. His short-term cash position will be favorable as a renter, and the true cost of living as a renter in the first year will be $18,000.

Case #2: Joe Converts a Duplex into a Single-family Residence

Many of Joe's friends and coworkers have recently purchased homes. Very few of those coworkers are purchasing half-duplexes, or small, reasonable condos. Instead, they purchase the largest, nicest single-family homes they can possibly qualify for. Sometimes, Joe suspects these folks are actually purchasing a little bit more home than they can afford.

Joe would like to fit in and believes he too can just barely qualify for (and afford) a mortgage to live in a large, nice single-family residence. In this case, he'd make some minor changes to the duplex by knocking out a wall and removing two doors to make it into a spacious single-family residence (SFR).

Joe's SFR assumptions:
- The property is listed at $300,000.
- The seller will cover the closing costs, and all costs needed to convert the property into an SFR (you might consider this the same as buying a typical nice-ish American SFR).
- Joe will put down the FHA minimum of 3.5 percent of the purchase price ($10,500).
- Joe's fixed interest rate will be 3.5 percent for a thirty-year mortgage.
- Joe's annual real estate taxes are 1 percent of the property's value.
- Joe's annual insurance payment is 1.5 percent of the property's value.
- Joe pays monthly FHA mortgage insurance, which comes to 1

percent of the initial loan amount.

- The property will appreciate with inflation at 3.4 percent per year.
- Joe will spend an average of $250 per month maintaining his home.
- For simplicity, Joe assumes in his model that he will claim standard tax deductions and not itemize interest or other loan costs.

Based on these assumptions, Joe realizes that purchasing the house and living in it as a homeowner is going to require way more cash up front than renting. He will have to put down $10,500 and will pay at least $29,000 in the first year in cash expenses for his mortgage, taxes, insurance, and upkeep. His cash outlay in the first year as a homeowner is close to $40,000.

At the same time, however, Joe is benefitting from average appreciation of about $10,200, and roughly $5600 of his mortgage payments will go toward paying down the loan— that contributes to his net worth. He also didn't "lose" the $10,500 he used that toward his down payment; it simply goes toward the equity in his property. These items offset his cash outlays and give him equity in the property, and the true cost of living (factoring in equity) as a homeowner in year one is roughly $13,400.

Case #3: Joe "Hacks" His Housing

Joe has recently heard about this new way to live, whereby he also buys as much housing as he can qualify for, but purchases it with the intent of buying a multifamily unit (like this duplex), living in one unit and renting out the other. He's intrigued by this so-called "house hacking" and suspects that it will lower his cost of living dramatically, though he can't be sure how impactful it will be until he runs the numbers. He understands his friends and coworkers will think he is slightly odd to live in a smaller space than he could afford, so the financial impact of this decision will have to be substantial.

Joe's house-hacking assumptions:
- All homeowner assumptions from Case 2 apply to the duplex.
- Joe will collect $18,000 per year or 0.5 percent of the property value per month in rent for half of the duplex.
- Rents will increase each year with inflation.
- Managing tenants in the other side will cost $100 per month

above and beyond the normal homeowner expenses of $250 per month, including vacancies.

- For simplicity, Joe will consider the yearly benefit of depreciation of the rental portion of the property to be offset by the capital gains taxes that will be due at sale, so Joe does not figure in these effects. (He also is aware that tax policies can change over time so he feels that making decisions today based on unknown future tax policies to be beyond his skill.)

Based on these assumptions, Joe sees that house hacking will cost him $40,836, including the down payment, in cash expenses in the first year, but that these cash costs will be offset by $18,000 collected in rent. In total, Joe's cash outlays (net of rent) for living will be $22,836 next year. Furthermore, like the homeowner, Joe also benefits from appreciation of $10,200 and $5608 in principal reduction, and of course, his $10,500 down payment doesn't count as lost wealth either. True cost of living as a house hacker in year one: negative $3368 (negative because he builds wealth!)

Joe's Conclusions

In just the first year, Joe's model tells him that living as a house hacker will result in building about $21,500 more wealth than the renter and about $16,800 more wealth than the homeowner. That's a huge amount of money, considering he earns a $50,000-per-year salary! Assuming he averages five hours a month managing his tenants next door (likely a *very* conservative estimate, most landlords will tell you they spend far less than this per month), that comes out to around $300 *per hour* for any efforts that a house hacker would have to put in over what a renter/homeowner would. Joe is unable to think of any other job that will pay him that kind of wage per hour, even if he is a legendary financial and spreadsheet whiz.

In an effort to visualize the wealth-building impact this decision will have on him over a longer period of time, Joe projected out and graphed the long-term impact of his three choices on his net worth build up and his annual cash outlay for this property. Joe came up with the following graphs:

Net Worth Impact 30 Years

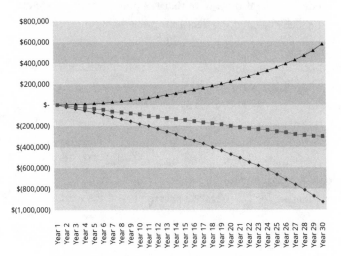

Cash Outlays for Living Next 30 Years

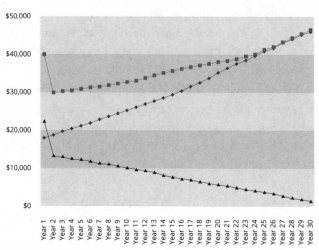

Over thirty years, Joe's model tells him that this decision's financial impact is almost beyond belief. Living as a house hacker will result in about $1.5 million more wealth than renting, and about $850,000 more wealth than buying an equivalent single family home. Yes, *not losing* wealth can be counted as *building wealth* in the case of housing, which for most people is one of those "fixed" expenses we discussed in chapter 2.

Interestingly, Joe notes that becoming a homeowner is a *losing invest-ment*. That's contrary to what most Americans think. True, it's *less bad* to own a home than to rent in scenarios like this one. But Joe will still lose close to $300,000 in wealth over thirty years just by living in his nice single-fam-ily residence. Plus, look at his cash outlays! His bank account will look way worse as a homeowner (less cash in the bank, more tied up in equity in his home) than if he were to just keep renting for the next twenty-five years! Even so, the results are clear: house hacking is so far and away the financial winner that it isn't even a comparison.

Costs of House Hacking

Joe's a pretty smart guy and doesn't forget to consider the subjective costs of house hacking. He knows that as a landlord, he will have to screen, vet, and address the issues that come up with his tenants. As a renter or home-owner, he won't have to do that. He also acknowledges he will be responsible for maintaining his house as either a homeowner *or* a house hacker. That's definitely less convenient than remaining a tenant and making the landlord do all that work. He recognizes that he has a tax liability when he sells the rental property, which will in part offset some of his gains. Finally, he acknowledges that house hacking is going to be slightly less awesome than living in a single family home with twice the available square footage (he'll only live in one of the two units, instead of a huge SFR, which might have twice as much living space for him).

Joe considers those costs, but he dismisses them systematically. He un-derstands that dealing with property management issues will be way easier for him than for any competing landlords or property managers—those guys actually have to get into their car and drive both themselves and their equipment to their rental properties, while his tenants are *right next door*.

He also accepts the duties that come with homeownership by reasoning he has no more responsibility in managing his home than any of the almost 75 million homeowners in the United States. Lastly, living space is a matter of priority. Joe reasons that since his unit would rent for $1500 per month, and this is almost twice the average national rent, that he can *still* live luxuriously, even in his favorite place in his favorite city. Living luxuriously, instead of living *really* luxuriously, is the price he will pay for the $850,000 he will make in his sleep over the next thirty years.

Joe's Next Steps

Joe is a savvy financial analyst and recognizes a good investment when he sees one. Joe immediately stops goofing around with the stock market, mutual funds, retirement accounts, and any of that other hogwash. A 200 percent return on investment is available! After all, you can be sure that any financier like Joe would consider a $20,000 increase in wealth on a $10,000 down payment, a 200 percent return on investment.

In fact, as a finance nerd, Joe will probably end up spending less time managing his property than he does attempting to pick winning stocks. There is just so clearly nothing else he can do with his money that's even remotely close to having as large a financial impact as house hacking will.

Joe's going to house hack. Are you?

Another Consideration

Joe couldn't help himself and had to factor yet another piece of the puzzle into his equations. You see, since the renter and the house hacker are spending *less cash* on their living situations than the homeowner, they have the opportunity to invest that cash in something else, like the stock market. In doing this, Joe is analyzing the *opportunity cost* of a lack of cash associated with the money needed in the first year to obtain the property.

If we extrapolate that every available dollar over and above what the SFR homebuyer will have available, is invested immediately in the stock market at 10 percent long-term returns, the picture changes in an interesting way. The renter actually has a leg-up on the homeowner from a cash position and has more cash to invest in the stock market. This lessens the true wealth gap between the renter, the house hacker, and the homeowner, and suggests that given the transaction costs of homeownership, it may be better to rent than to buy in the short-medium term. The homeowner has the least amount of cash available, since most of his wealth is tied up in equity in his property. This results in less opportunity to invest and makes owning a home even less favorable.

The house hacker has the lowest cash outlay over time (although not in year one, compared to the renter, as he has to put down $10,500 to buy the property), and thus his net worth accelerates over the long term as he plows that extra cash into other investments. The differences, calculated in this manner, can be seen below and further support the conclusions drawn previously.

Net Worth Impact with Cash Savings Reinvested 30 Years

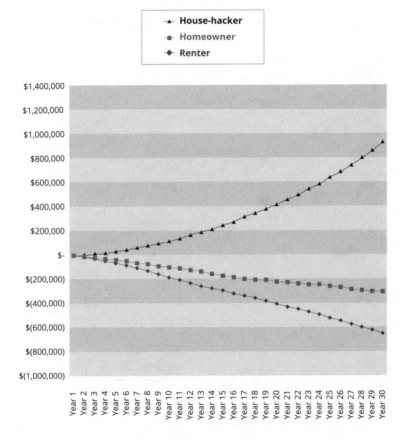

Only in rare circumstances will house hacking prove to be less financially beneficial than renting. Perhaps only in the two or three most expensive cities in the nation will *no* purchasing options be reasonably available to the median earner. And, it would take a very unique set of circumstances for buying a property as a single-family residence to prove more financially advantageous than buying a similarly priced property house-hacking style.

Conclusion

House hacking is an extremely important wealth-building step for the median wage earner with near typical spending patterns. The reason you save so aggressively in part I is to put yourself in position to easily take advantage of the tactic of house hacking. It's an incredibly powerful way to eradicate one of the largest expenses in your life and replace wealth destruction with wealth creation. But it's far easier to pull off for the guy with excellent credit, excess cash to pay for unexpected problems, and a strong savings rate to get through the occasional month without tenant or roommate assistance. Don't skip straight to this part. Build your financial foundation one step at a time.

Chapter 5
The Financial Impact of Housing Decisions

Housing is the largest expense for many Americans. In the last chapter, you saw how someone earning a median salary with just $10,500 saved cannot only wipe out this expense entirely, but actually *build wealth* with his or her housing. There are very few financial decisions more impactful than this one for full-time nine-to-five wage earners interested in early financial freedom. Those who fail to house hack are missing out on perhaps the most powerful wealth-building tool available to ordinary Americans.

However, not everyone will house hack for reasons specific to their personal situations, or because they have short-term lifestyle goals that are prioritized above and beyond early financial freedom. The purpose of this chapter, then, is to demonstrate the continuum of home purchase decisions, and their corresponding impact on early financial freedom.

There are five general ways the average Americans can buy their first homes. Each way has different short and long-term financial consequences.

Five Ways to Buy a First Property and Their Financial Consequences

Way #1: Buying a Luxury Home

This type of purchase involves buying the most expensive home one can possibly qualify for. It involves stretching one's self to the absolute financial limits to own the best possible piece of real estate in the best possible location. It's the most destructive way to purchase a property, and sadly, it's also very common.

Sally is a twenty-seven-year-old hard-working young professional with an excellent job, making approximately $80,000 per year. She used her life savings of $25,000 toward the down payment on a $425,000 luxury condo overlooking the city and right next to the big sports stadium. Sally thought this was a good investment because condos in that part of town are the most in-demand in the city, and she thinks that this type of property "always goes up!" Sally had a killer housewarming party and invited all her friends over.

Three years in, Sally finds that prices have only risen modestly, and that she can no longer afford to keep up the fancy vacations she took as a renter, regularly upgrade her car every year or two, and go out to her favorite restaurants with the frequency that she was used to. Rising HOA fees, coupled with the already expensive mortgage force her to continually sacrifice in other areas of her life. Meanwhile, another new complex was recently built with far more in-demand condos than hers. Friends no longer want to go to her place to hang out, and instead go to another friend's condo in the newer, fancier building.

Tom and Nancy are a thirty-four-year-old couple with an infant son and a daughter on the way. Combined they had a household income of about $130,000, and purchased a $650,000 home in the best school district in their city. They used their entire life savings, outside of their retirement funds, toward the down payment, and borrowed a little money from Nancy's father to help cover the rest. They believed they were planning for their children's futures. They believed this was a good investment because "the schools are so good and we've got such a great view."

A few years later, Tom and Nancy are finally back to being able to save up some money. It's been a tough few years. They can never seem to save money, maintaining their property is a lot more work than they thought, and prices haven't risen as much as they thought they would. They are stuck for at least a couple more years in their house. Tom was recently offered a job that paid significantly more in a city much closer to Tom and Nancy's parents. Unfortunately, Nancy can't get a job that pays anywhere near her current salary in the new city, so Tom has to decline the job. It's a shame too, because Nancy would have liked to stay home with the children, but right now they just can't afford to move because they can't sell the house.

Who knows if another opportunity like this will come Tom's way?

This is the dream, right? Work hard in school, get a good job, get married, save up, and then you can buy the house with the white picket fence on top of the hill and send your kids to the best schools that your region has to offer. Unfortunately, this is also a quick way into the middle-class American Dream graveyard. This type of first-time home purchase is often accompanied with financial choices such as:

- Putting all of one's savings, outside of retirement accounts, into the home

- Borrowing for the down payment from friends and family

- Using over a third of one's after-tax take-home pay to cover the mortgage

This type of person espouses benefits to buying this type of property such as:

- Getting to live in the cool part of town

- Sending one's kids to the best schools

- Central location, accessibility to highways and cities

This type of purchase is so sought after because the people who purchase this type of home or condo have the coolest housewarming parties, the biggest smiles, and the most jealous friends and colleagues. People think that folks who purchase property of this type must be doing something right. Why then, is this such a bad plan?

When folks stretch themselves to their financial limits to buy property, they sacrifice almost everything else. In effect, they *mortgage away virtually every other financial decision they can make in life*. Here are some consequences of this choice:

- Your career. You know that place where you spend most of the hours of your day, most of the days of the week, most of the weeks of the year, most of the years of your life? That place? Yep, you lose almost all flexibility in career decisions when you stretch yourself to buy property. You have only two choices: stay at your current job or a very similar one that pays very similarly in your current city, or hope for a massive raise and huge signing bonus to help you out if you want to move elsewhere.

- The stability of your financial position. Because you stretched yourself to your financial limit to qualify for the loan, and until you get a raise, you're basically paycheck-to-paycheck maintaining the status quo. Furthermore, you *will* be hit with unexpected and irregular maintenance expenses as the owner of real estate, and if you are unable to save up, these irregular maintenance expenses become disasters.

- Entertainment expenses. Because you deplete your cash position and incur greater monthly payments, if you stretch yourself to your financial limits to buy a primary residence you may find that you have to cut out other lifestyle choices like eating out, vacations, new cars, etc.

- Relaxation time. Your relaxation time is limited partially because of financial reasons listed above, and partially due to the fact that you have to spend more *time* maintaining your home than you did previously as a renter. You surely can't afford to outsource maintenance in this position.

In spite of the rather obvious consequences of buying property like this, folks do this all the time. They intentionally gravitate to this type of transaction, ignoring all of the negative consequences listed above, and put themselves in a weak long-term financial position dictated by the values of real estate in their local market.

Remember too that just because you're buying a "reasonable" property that's not in the ludicrously expensive part of town, doesn't mean the property is reasonable for *you*. If the most you can possibly qualify for is $300,000, then you're guilty of buying in this manner if you buy a $300,000 property. It's the same financial and decision-making effect as the guy stretching himself to the max buying a $750,000 home.

This way of purchasing is one of the most foolish financial decisions you can make if you are pursuing early financial freedom. The most frustrating part about all this is that often the folks doing this type of buying have the biggest egos, and when prices go up, they boast about what was really a reckless decision. They would never admit they got lucky! Sure, they suffered the consequences above, and had to work harder than they imagined to stay afloat, but in the end, here they are sitting on equity and able to sell at a profit.

The problem is this way of buying only works out favorably if the buyer experiences rapid appreciation or if the buyer earns significantly more income shortly after the purchase. By the way, even if the market does shoot up, folks who purchase property in this manner would be in a far stronger financial position if they'd bought property in a more intelligent way. Unfortunately, if the market appreciates only modestly, or declines, the buyer of this type of property is out of luck, and they have no way out.

In short, stretching yourself to your financial limits to buy a primary residence is a foolish, easily preventable mistake that will cost you dearly in your ability to make future decisions. If you knowingly choose to forgo most future opportunity beyond maintaining the status quo, the desirability of that piece of real estate had better be incredible. You should understand that by purchasing that property, you are willingly sacrificing pretty much every other area of life that money can impact over the next five to ten years.

Don't buy the most expensive piece of real estate in the most expensive area with your first home purchase if you aspire to early financial freedom. Don't lock yourself into a mortgage and physical location that limits your freedom for the foreseeable future. You never know what might happen in a few years, and retaining the option to move without dire financial consequences can put you at a huge advantage. Instead, buy a home that affords you the luxury of future choice.

Way #2: Buying a Reasonable Home

This type of purchase is one in which folks buy a home that is well within their means. Reasons like, "I felt like it was time to buy," or "I'm tired of paying rent" often accompany these purchase decisions. While it's more conservative than purchasing the most expensive piece of real estate possible, this type of purchase can also have long-lasting financial consequences that leave the buyer at the mercy of the market and needlessly delay early financial freedom.

> *Jeff was tired of paying rent, and had been responsible with his money for a long time. After working hard for about four years, he had a solid nest egg of $35,000, and decided to put $20,000 toward the purchase of a decent condo in his city. He qualified for up to $400,000 in financing, but decided he was more comfortable with properties in the $300,000 range as that would put less pressure on his budget and allow him to save more. After living in the property for a few years, Jeff met a wonderful young lady, and they decided to get married and start a family in her hometown. Jeff sold his property for a modest gain, and moved onto the next stage of his life in a new city.*

Abby and Jared were ready to start a family and decided it was time to move to a home of their own. They made a combined $120,000 per year and had $50,000 saved up. While their lender told them they could qualify for a property in the $700,000 range, they decided to purchase something far more reasonable in the $400,000 range. They knew it wasn't the best school district, but figured that they could save far more money in a more modest property, and if they found the schools unsuitable, could move when their unborn children reached school age. A few years later, Abby and Jared unexpectedly have triplets, and the home they purchased is no longer suitable. They sell their home and just about break even, and then buy a slightly larger property with room for their new, unexpectedly large family.

Many conservative folks who don't run the numbers or who don't have a long-term outlook on their financial positions buy property in this manner. These people are in much better position to handle life decisions than in folks that buy a luxury home as in Way #1 above. But while they will not expose themselves to as much pressure as folks who stretch to their financial limits, they aren't getting ahead either. They still shell out a large amount of cash with the down payment, take on a mortgage, and have to maintain their property. However, people who buy more reasonably are protected in down or steady markets. They have more exit options, and aren't so stretched that they lose all flexibility in other parts of their lives.

For those seeking early financial freedom, buying property that's reasonably affordable is a better bet than buying expensive property. The owner will come out a little bit ahead of renting an equivalent unit assuming they stay there a long period of time. However, "affordable" is relative. Someone who makes $250,000 per year might find a $750,000 to be quite within the comforts of their budget, while someone who makes $50,000 per year might be stretched with a $350,000 purchase. It is up to you to determine if you can *easily* afford the payments on a property, and have plenty of cash on hand to handle problems as they come up.

Way #3: Buying a Home the Smart Way

This type of purchase involves buying a property that's very affordable. It also involves thinking through the exit strategies and possibilities that may come up later. The smart home buyer will buy a place that's well within their

district. Using the rent from their friendly, handpicked neighbors living in the other side, they're able to save very quickly.

Because they have the tenant's rent helping to cover their mortgage, just three years later, Drew and Carol are able to afford a more expensive triplex in the very best school district in the state. Their kids enter middle school in the best possible situation, and unlike their peers, Drew and Carol are able to afford to live in the area while taking a family vacation every year. Carol even recently quit her job to have more time with the kids. Drew and Carol do not earn higher salaries than their neighbors, it's just that their entire housing situation, and maybe a little extra, is covered by the rents from their duplex and the two other units in their new triplex.

House hacking is the optimal financial decision for most first-time buyers. As Joe showed us in the last chapter, house hacking entails buying a piece of investment real estate with the intention of living in it, while renting portion(s) of the property to cover the mortgage payments. This enables the owner to live for free or for much less than other local homeowners or renters. It's like benefitting from all the advantages of homeownership without the mortgage payment. It is also likely to be far safer than renting, regular home ownership, or buying investment property like a real estate investor.

House hacking rewards first-time buyers in almost every short and long-term financial area, and offers flexibility in their decision-making process that's far superior to peers purchasing property in some of the other ways discussed earlier. The house hacker can live in the property indefinitely, can sell the property at will, or can turn it into an excellent income-producing asset. That combination of choices is rarely available to first-time homeowners who choose one of the other ways described above.

Taking the next step, a house hack should *make sense as an investment property at the time of purchase.* You put yourself in an advantageous position if you buy an investment property that a professional real estate investor might consider. Furthermore, house hacking can be combined with the live-in-flip strategy discussed earlier. It's quite feasible to buy an investment property that needs some work, fix it up, increasing both the value of the property and the rent that it can command. This offers the purchaser an advantageous situation!

The house hacker even gets the added benefit of choosing his neighbors!

In many cases, folks moving into new areas are cautious about the types of people in their neighborhoods. As long as you aren't discriminating illegally, you can choose the kindest, quietest neighbors who apply and kick out (either by evicting or refusing to renew a lease) the ones you don't like. It's just like owning a townhome, except with the ability to pick your neighbors, and with the bonus of being able to use the rent you collect to cover the mortgage payment.

Like the ways above, house hacking can involve buying the newest and nicest set of townhomes in the best part of the city, or buying property with more value-added opportunities. The house hacker looking for a fancy place in a nice part of town and prioritizing a high-end lifestyle will get one return, while the house hacker looking for a value-added potential and the ability to generate lots of rent, relative to the purchase price, will get another return. Both will be better off than their counterparts who rent or buy outright. House hacking is especially promising for young men and women who are willing to live in transitioning neighborhoods and fix up properties all on their own, and families willing to live in decent multifamily properties where their kids can still go to excellent schools.

By this point you should have a clear understanding of the consequences of buying property the way most Americans do. Millions of Americans think they are living the dream when they buy the biggest, fanciest, best-situated property they can afford. But that purchase comes at the cost of other dreams. Few are able to save significant portions of their earned income with 30 percent or more of their income going just to their mortgage payment. These people will have a shorter financial runway and large monthly upkeep expenses thanks to their "lovely" homes. Don't do this to yourself. Wait until you are well on your way or have arrived at early financial freedom, and *then* use the passive income from your first or second starter homes or house hacks to cover a mortgage payment on a long-term residence. Don't cripple yourself financially right from the beginning!

Questions to Ask Before Buying a House Hack

Assuming you understand the merits of house hacking, especially as a first home purchase during the initial years of wealth building, this section will show you how to make a great purchase. There are four questions that savvy first-time house hackers should ask themselves prior to buying a home or house hack:

1. Is the property affordable with conventional financing?

2. Are you willing to live in the property?

3. Will the property cash flow?

4. Is there a reasonable chance at appreciation?

It's easy to house hack and come out better than an average renter or regular homeowner in almost every city in the country. It can be difficult, however, to buy a cash flowing rental property in a specific part of town that the buyer really wants to live in. The truly difficult problem is in deciding *where* to make that commitment. Buying a rental property with the intention of living in it and actively managing it is more than just a financial commitment. The buyer is going to live, work, and invest in that area for the next few years at least. Here's how to answer those four questions:

Question #1: Is the Property Affordable with Conventional Financing?

There are two obvious follow-up questions to the "Can I afford this?" question:

- How much money do you have?

- How much money does property in the area you want to buy cost?

Those looking to purchase their first property will need some cash to make the transaction work, and it might not be as much as you think. Some folks think they need to save 20 percent of the purchase price of a home, or more. That's not true. Folks with good credit and a good job can put down as little as 3.5 percent using an FHA loan. On a $300,000 property that's just $10,500.

However, prior to buying a first home or house hack, in addition to the down payment, you'll want to have accumulated thousands or tens of thousands of dollars. This extra cash will help you cover any problems that might come up like repairs and maintenance issues. So, while you don't need to accumulate $60,000 in cash to buy your first $300,000 home or house hack, you will want to structure the purchase in such a way that you retain at least five figures in wealth that can be accessed to take care of potential problems. See why the goal of part I is the accumulation of the first $25,000?

Question #2: Are You Willing to Live in the Property?

The purchase of a primary residence or house hack doesn't meet a basic lifestyle goal if you are unhappy living there. Buy in a location that's acceptable to you and makes sense, given the other things going on in your life. If your city is too expensive, figure out what you need to do to put yourself in a financial position to purchase reasonable investment property, move to another city, or expand your search radius.

Fortunately, many cities have surrounding neighborhoods with properties at price points affordable to folks making around $50,000 per year. These neighborhoods are often convenient to downtown with good bike routes and cab/Uber rides downtown that are less than $10 a pop. Find one of those areas. If your city doesn't offer property that meets these criteria you will have to move to another city or understand that your personal choice to remain in one of the few, extremely expensive cities in the country will significantly delay your financial freedom.

Question #3: Will the Property Cash Flow?

There are two cash flow analyses that you will want to perform on the purchase of a primary residence. The first analysis will be the cash flow with you as an occupant. The second will be the cash flow without you as an occupant. A true house hack should be analyzed like an investment property. It should produce cash flow so that if you moved away and hired someone else to manage it, it would generate reliable passive income for you.

Envision a cheap duplex listed for $240,000 in a reasonable part of town. Each half of this duplex rents for $1200 per month, $2400 in total. With an FHA loan, this property might have a mortgage payment including principal, interest, taxes, and insurance of about $1500 per month. Some additional expenses include:

- Repairs and maintenance, $50 per month
- Water, gas, electric, and sewer, $180 per month
- Capital expenditures (large irregular expenditures), $200 per month
- Vacancies at 5 percent of rent, $120 per month
- Property management (buyer moves away and can't manage herself), $200 per month

In this case, the property would generate $2400 per month in income as a standalone investment, and would have $2250 in expenses, if the owner were to move away. This property produces a small amount of cash flow per month, and will allow the owner a great deal of flexibility if she needs to move.

While the owner is living there, this property will have lower vacancy, repairs, and maintenance costs, and no property management expense, because the owner has read part I of this book and takes care of basic tasks do-it-yourself style. In fact, the entire labor cost of those types of repairs will be eliminated, leaving the owner with just the cost of materials. But, the owner will also be collecting rent only from one side of the property. In this case, the owner will have closer to $1800 in expenses, offset by $1200 in rent. While that's still an average of $600 per month leaving the owner's pocket, it is clearly far superior to renting or the expenses of owning a property without a tenant offsetting part of the cost.

Question #4: Is There a Reasonable Chance at Appreciation?

If you read up on real estate investing and buying homes, you'll learn experienced investors refer to appreciation as the "icing on the cake"—it's usually not even a major consideration in the purchase of an investment property. While it's still a good idea to look at cash-flow first as an owner-occupier, putting in the extra time to look for investment properties that offer a good chance at appreciation as well can reward you handsomely in the long run.

As a live-in house hacker—because of a special tax law that benefits owner-occupiers—appreciation can produce a more powerful financial impact for you than it can for a traditional investor. *Assuming you live in the property for more than two years, when you sell the property, much of the capital gains are tax-free.* This tax break is incredibly powerful for those looking to house hack with small multifamily properties because you have the opportunity to take advantage of appreciation as it relates to both income properties and smaller residential properties: For multi-family properties, increasing the *income* of the property can force appreciation as investors will pay more money for a property with more rent.

As hybrid properties, duplexes to fourplexes can also benefit from appreciation caused by an improving local market. Try to select a property that offers a blend of opportunity:

- Forced Income Appreciation: Adding value to a property is a spectrum containing everything from completely dilapidated properties to properties that just need a new paint job. If you choose a property with some easy opportunities for improvement, you may be able to get a great deal or add value quickly and cheaply. This can increase your equity and/or allow you to charge more for rent.

- Market Appreciation: One of the benefits to purchasing property in an area that you yourself want to live in is that generally speaking, other folks will want to live there too. This presents a decent opportunity for appreciation in and of itself if you have personal reasons for desiring to live in a certain area that also apply to other demographics. Pay attention to what's going on in the local area, and buy property that's in a transitioning part of town, or that's likely to benefit from new projects.

A homebuyer or house hacker that can benefit from both types of appreciation will make huge financial progress in a short period of time. If just some of these results are produced, then the buyer may find himself with the option to cash out on that equity largely tax-free or tax-deferred, and reinvest it in a larger income producing real estate asset.

Conclusion

A house hack is applicable to an incredibly broad range of Americans. The answer to the traditional "buy vs. rent" debate typically (but not always) plays out to the tune of "buying is better if you plan to live there for several years, renting is better in the short run." Well, if that's true, then house hacking simply rapidly accelerates the break-even point in favor of the buyer. If you are more than a few years away from financial independence, there are likely to be few more obvious decisions to make than house hacking to expedite the process.

If you buy a rental property that would cash flow from day one and house hack it, you should have far more flexibility in a year or two than your peers that are renting, not less. You are *not* committing to the area you are buying in. In fact, you are *less* tied to the area, financially speaking, than an average homeowner *and* a renter.

How come? Because your property would cash flow as an investment property if you moved out! You don't have a lease with yourself, you can move across town, or across the country, as soon as you find some new tenants to move in. A tenant must fulfill the terms of the lease prior to vacating a property, meaning that decisions are made with the lease term in mind. An owner can move out and put a tenant in place any time they please.

Buying income producing real estate as a primary residence can have the immediate effect of drastically reducing or eliminating your housing costs and boosting your savings rate, *and* gives you the potential to benefit from appreciation if you are in a market that's desirable. Really, there's no question that this strategy is a good one for a large number of people, in a wide variety of markets.

It is up to you to decide: *Is your first home going to set yourself up for a life of financial abundance? Or, is living in the nicest largest, best-located home you can possibly afford in the short-term more important than all of the other financial decisions you can make today, and that you might make down the line?*

Turn your first home into an income-producing asset, and make an incredible leap forward.

Chapter 6
How to Make More Money

This is the part everyone always wants to skip to. Everyone is interested in learning how to make more money. Everyone wants a shortcut to earning a high salary. It is inefficient to focus too heavily on income production prior to making efficient lifestyle choices as they pertain to spending, particularly with regards to housing. But, a house hacker living for free and living a frugal lifestyle overall will cease to benefit from further reduction in expenses.

If you feel you're extremely frugal, living a life far removed from the median American's high spending patterns, then further cuts to your budget might be detrimental to your actual enjoyment of life. If that's the case, and you are prepared to make still more changes in pursuit of financial freedom, then now is the time to start focusing earnestly on increasing your income.

Remember, this chapter, like the rest of this book, is written for folks in a very specific set of circumstances. The individual who benefits from this yearns to rapidly move toward early financial freedom. She works a wage-paying job about which she may not be passionate. She may not actively despise her work, but she would not show up if money were no longer a concern. Furthermore, she is willing to make significant lifestyle changes and work exceptionally hard to more rapidly achieve her goal of early financial freedom.

There are millions of people out there who love their work, and who perform rewarding and valuable services that benefit our communities and the nation. They might be content to work those jobs for essentially forever. This chapter isn't written for those folks. If you love your job in a field like healthcare, education, military or public services, or countless other professions that keep our country safe or provide for the general well-being, then I thank you for your service. It should be clear however, that opportunities for rapid salary increases in those lines of work are unlikely. A job without opportunity for rapid salary advancement doesn't offer the opportunity for the rapid attainment of financial freedom. If your career path is one that is unlikely to lead to a high income, you will need to pursue early financial freedom simply through frugality and on-the-side investing, and make progress on the income front where you can in your free time.

Instead, this chapter is written purposefully for the young, ambitious employee (or soon to be college graduate) who feels their talents may be underutilized and underpaid. This is written for the fellow who doesn't find particular joy in his career or line of work.

Fundamental to this approach is the concept of *transitioning out of your current job* (or even career) and into a set of working conditions in which there is a reasonable likelihood of increasing your income to an upper-middle class level and beyond.

Personally, I started my career as a financial analyst at a Fortune 500 company. It took me less than three months to understand that type of work wasn't something I wanted to do with the rest of my twenties, much less the rest of my career. It took me another three months to figure out there was also very little potential on the income front. So, what did I do? I quit my $50,000 per year job to pursue my dream of early financial freedom and real estate investing. I joined a tiny startup with just two employees and joined the tech industry, using my financial background as an entry point. I took a pay cut at the time, so that I could have exposure to opportunity (I manage sales for the company at the time of this writing). As a result of this change, and a ton of hard work, I was able to triple my salary in just two years.

While this is possible for anyone, this process is significantly less risky for those who have completed the objective in part I, have no bad debts, live frugally, and have at least a year's worth of expenses at the ready.

If you are unable to satisfy these conditions and lack around a year of financial runway you may forgo some (but certainly not all) of the opportunities available to increase your income substantially. It is much easier to take a small pay cut with a year of financial runway than it is with little to nothing saved. Just as it is easy to take a large pay cut or work entirely for commissions with many years of financial runway built up. If you do pursue larger income without a financial cushion to fall back on, you risk financial consequences, like falling into debt.

What Is the Point of Earning More Money?

As it pertains to the goal of early financial freedom, the point of earning more money is so that it can be used to acquire income-producing assets. The point of everything in this book is to rapidly bring about early financial freedom. The point isn't to purchase more trinkets, or to support a lavish lifestyle. Those who desire income to live a lavish lifestyle will find that the strategy for increasing one's income outlined here is disadvantageous. This plan may actually result in a short-term *reduction* in disposable income—at least at first—in many cases.

The point of earning more money is to enable you to *keep more money,* so that it can be *invested* according to an appropriately-tailored plan, in a manner which is reasonably likely to produce usable net worth and spendable passive income to fund early financial freedom. Do not concern yourself with immediate income opportunity in the form of the highest base salary. Instead, ask yourself which jobs, opportunities, and careers offer the potential for income in the next three to five years. Remember, the goal isn't to earn more money *immediately*, but to pursue opportunities that are likely to offer you the ability to rapidly and consistently scale far beyond your current level of income, helping you to reach your financial goals far sooner than you might otherwise be able to.

How to Make Time to Pursue More Income

Fundamental to increasing one's income is spending the appropriate time on high impact tasks that are likely to produce scalable income. So, how can you make time to focus on earning more income?

A wage earning employee trades their time for money, so it is through a more efficient and productive use of time this employee will be able to earn more money and escape the rat race. Therefore, the wage earner who wishes to rapidly increase their income must carefully analyze how they make use of their time to ensure they are spending it as efficiently as possible in the pursuit of more income. If they are not spending their time improving their financial positions, then they had better be enjoying it or serving others. Otherwise, they are wasting time.

Remember Average Joe? Average Joe, aside from being kind enough to share his $50,000 salary, spending, and housing preferences with us, has also shared how he spends his time on an average work day. Those interested in learning how to track their time will be offered a method for doing so in chapter 12. In this chapter, we will break down how Average Joe spends his workday, and look for the biggest areas where we can make an impact on Joe's prospects. For our study, we will again use data from the federal government, shown in the pie chart below.

Time use on an average work day for employed persons ages 25 to 54 with children

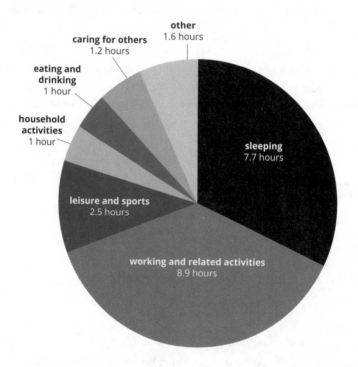

NOTE: Data include employed persons on days they worked, ages 25 to 54, who lived in households with children under 18. Data include non-holiday weekdays and are annual averages for 2014. Data include related travel for each activity.
SOURCE: Bureau of Labor Statistics, American Time Use Survey

Note first that a large chunk of the graph is time spent asleep. While there are some folks out there who attempt to eat away at that chunk of the pie, this book isn't going to offer an opinion on that subject. For our purposes, let's assume that Average Joe cannot use the time he spends sleeping on more productive pursuits. Instead, let's analyze on how he can apply his waking hours most effectively in the pursuit of generating additional income. The largest chunk of the graph is "working and related activities" which can be summed up as "work plus commute" for the Average Joe. The total time spent here is about 8.9 hours per day.

After work and commuting, the remaining third of the graph is comprised of the following:

- Leisure and sports. The largest part of Joe's leisure time is generally spent watching TV or consuming video content through another medium.

- Eating and drinking. While Joe might be able to scarf his food down with greater rapidity, there's probably not much room for improvement in this category.

- Household activities. Average Joe might be able to operate more efficiently here, but if he has a family or enjoys a clean and orderly lifestyle, he will have to keep house.

- Caring for others. Joe isn't so obsessed with the pursuit of early financial freedom that he leaves his friends and family out to dry when they need him, so there's no room for improvement here.

- Other. Every Average Joe is an individual and has quirks and pleasures that need to be addressed on an individual basis.

Let's address the elephant in the room. Which slice of this graph is the largest? Which slice of this graph represents over 50 percent of one's waking hours? Which slice of this graph is holding Average Joe back from earning more income?

Obviously, it's his *work and commute*. Yes, there is room for improvement. Yes, Joe could stop watching Netflix for two hours each night. Yes, Joe could probably cut some of the fat from his other activities and run a more efficient evening. Yes, Joe could develop a routine that's more efficient. But all this pales in comparison to the possibilities available to Joe if he could spend his workday pursuing more income.

This is the problem with those other books that suggest starting a "side hustle" or taking on a second job as the appropriate first step toward earning more income. This approach is like trying to get rich by cutting out happy hour or weekly date night. It's possible it could work for those with an obvious opportunity or problem they need to tackle in order to build wealth. But, nine-to-fivers just don't have *time* in material quantities outside their work. It is laughably inefficient to try to make one's fortune in 5 percent to

10 percent of their time.

Additionally, time differs from money in one very important way—not all time has the same value to Joe. If Joe's loved ones are only available and alert during certain hours of the day, or if Joe performs best during certain parts of the day, then those hours are *more important* than other hours. This is completely different than money, where a dollar is a dollar (as long as it is after tax!) no matter where it goes. Saving money in one form is just as advantageous as saving it in another form. All time isn't created equal.

The period in which Average Joe is most likely to be alert and productive is the period containing and surrounding the typical nine to five workday. Regardless of individual preference, those eight hours are when most other businesses are open, and when most income-producing opportunities materialize. A morning person still has to wait until 9:00 a.m. to visit the bank, just as a night owl will find it closed after 5:00 p.m. While everyone is different with their personal productivity preferences, employers aren't paying for groggy and unproductive employees. They have their staff at work during the part of the day where they are likely to be thinking and working most efficiently. The obvious conclusion drawn from the available data and countless individual examples is this: You'll need to have the opportunity to earn more and more money available during the workday if you want to efficiently scale your income. You'll need to change your job and likely your career if you want to earn significantly more money significantly faster than you will on your current career track. Thus, salaried, specialized work is the worst kind of work in America today for the ambitious seeker of early financial freedom looking to scale her income. This is especially true in traditional industries like finance, accounting, consulting, corporate ladder-type roles, marketing, and basically anything and everything you might enter into that promises a steady paycheck in exchange for experience with a specific skillset.

The Problem with a Good Salaried Job

If you work a wage-paying job and earn a median salary, you will not scale your income by continuing to do what you are doing. Let's demonstrate this by looking at a typical career track for a young finance professional at a Fortune 500 company:

↓ Associate Financial Analyst: $48,000/yr. for one to two years

↓ Financial Analyst I: $55,000/yr. for one to two years

- ↓ Financial Analyst II: $62,000/yr. for one to two years

- ↓ Senior Financial Analyst: $71,000/yr. for one to two years

- ↓ Finance Manager: $84,000/yr. for one to two years

- ↓ Senior Finance Manager: $93,000/yr. for one to two years

- ↓ Director of Finance: $107,000/yr. for one to two years

- ↓ Senior Finance Director: $122,000/yr. for one to two years

- ↓ VP of Finance: $145,000/yr. for one to two years

- ↓ Senior VP of Finance: $165,000/yr. for one to two years

- ↓ CFO: $250,000+/yr. for 5+ years

This is an example of an extremely successful career with fairly rapid advancement. Within twenty years, a young college graduate has become the CFO of a major international corporation, and earns an enormous paycheck. Can you spot the flaw, however? It's that *within twenty years* part. Remember, this is the best-case scenario. In reality, most people in this profession are not able to succeed at this fantastic rate and rise to CFO of a Fortune 500 company in less than twenty years.

Sure, there are some bonuses that are likely to be involved, and the value of the benefits might kick in later in the career. But, this career track *guarantees* that the best-case scenario is one in which you will not earn more than $100,000 in salary for the first ten years or so.

Corporations dictate this career path and advancement relies on the recommendation of superiors. The goal of this corporation and superiors isn't for the analyst to be successful. It's for the team to be successful. That means that the ambitious rising star needs to be squashed back down into place. A junior analyst with just a few years experience cannot have a title and salary beyond that of more senior folks! That's preposterous, would hurt morale, and might put the structure of the organization at risk.

What matters in this world is years of experience. It's an incredibly rare feat even for outperformers to rise to a senior position like director or VP in a traditional branch of a large corporation in less than ten years. Why not pursue a career track that's more fun and more profitable? Do not allow some subjective manager to determine your financial future with a performance review that corresponds to a tiny annual raise.

Instead, those looking to dramatically increase their income will have to be compensated for performance against an objective metric. In many corporations, skilled professionals do what they are asked day in and day out for years. Their core competencies closely resemble the skillset of thousands or millions of other workers, and thus, they are denied the opportunity for rapid advancement. Workers quickly accept the rules of this game, and produce excellent work in a narrow area in the hopes they will please their direct superiors. They don't take on additional work on a volunteer basis, and attempt to appear busy, so that they aren't assigned additional work just to keep them occupied for the entire day.

Why? Because they aren't rewarded for producing more than the next guy. In fact, going above and beyond in a salaried job often results in a punishment. What happens to the team member who can handle twice as much work as the next guy? Well, he's given twice as much work! Is he paid twice as much? Heavens, no. Pay, of course, isn't based on productivity, but instead is based on experience. It reflects tenure in the form of years of service to the company or in the industry. They call it "paying your dues."

Of course, when the job is on the line, these folks shape up and quickly pick up whatever workload is necessary to maintain their position. But in the good times, this kind of work environment destroys ambition. Wage-earning employees learn, through years or decades of experience not to try too hard. They learn to do their jobs, not ask too many hard questions, put on a polite and pleasant appearance each day in the office, complete the tasks they've been assigned within the timelines provided, and go home. Some of them even think that the appropriate way to build wealth is to put in "butt time" by sitting at their cubicles for long hours throughout the better part of their twenties and early thirties.

Coupled with a personal finance outlook seeking to spend every penny they earn, a startling pattern emerges. A surprisingly large number of Americans become unmotivated, specialized, unhealthy, and dependent on their current jobs to make it through the short-term future. They learn to passively accept the workday, and are too tired and unmotivated from their week to do anything other than watch a little bit of TV and go on the occasional weekend trip to visit the in-laws. What a terrible way to approach a career. But, does it sound familiar?

This slow drain of enthusiasm and ambition confines your hunger for achievement to little wins one can earn from the cubicle. March Madness bracket becomes exceedingly important. Fantasy football becomes a central part of the workday banter. People jockey for the corporate tickets to the ball game. Wearing the stupidest tie in the office on Wednesdays is something of a weekly contest. Folks plan out ways to sneakily be the first one out of the parking lot at 4:00 p.m. on the dot on Friday. They apply their best creative efforts to these things—and it's because creativity is slowly suffocated in a salaried job!

Living out a professional life over decades in this manner is a terrible fate that those who achieve early financial freedom can avoid easily. Yet it seems to be the fate of the majority of intelligent white-collar workers! What do the best educated, most accomplished individuals do with their careers? Exactly this. That's right, most of *the best* competition out there is earning a high wage, with little opportunity to flex their talents in a wide variety of business pursuits. Their abilities, ambition, and drive are slowly being suffocated and destroyed. They have no control over what they do, beyond the narrow confines of completing certain types of assignments in certain ways, as directed by their superiors.

The guys who are starting businesses, building empires, growing portfolios, traveling the world, and succeeding by all conventional measures of success aren't doing so by being smarter than the average person. They are winning because they are playing a game where the possibility of success actually exists! It's a game where they have at least a little control over their workday and productivity! Play that game! Not the one where winning means making your boss laugh.

How to Earn More Money

Much like frugality, increased earning potential must be pursued by dissecting one's resources and ruthlessly cutting out the fat. This chapter presents advice that's just as personal, and just as directly impactful to major life decisions as the chapter on designing a frugal lifestyle. Those looking to earn more money, like those looking to save more money, are going to have to do some things that may be uncomfortable or new. They are going to have to make changes and perform actions that may not pay off for months or even years. They are going to have to make some big changes to their lifestyle and to their careers. Regular folks without the goal of early financial freedom will not understand these actions, or the reasons behind them.

None of this should be a surprise, and the validity of the points should be self-evident, even if some parts of this plan may not be feasibly implemented in the immediate future. Furthermore, unlike the discussion on cutting back on spending, none of these changes are a guarantee. This isn't a "step-by-step guide to making over $100,000 per year" in the same way that the section on frugality *was* a step-by-step guide to saving $25,000 in a year. Sales and objective performance are never guarantees in the way that refusing to spend $10 on a beer at the ball game guarantees retention of $10. Instead, income is increased when folks take deliberate action to improve a metric and are paid objectively or develop a skill that's highly sought after.

Changes Necessary to Increase One's Income

There are three simple things that median wage earners can do in order to sell their time and their talents for more income:

1. Develop highly sought-after skills.

2. Take control of one's future income.

3. Find synergies between one's work and lifestyle and investments.

Step #1: Develop Highly Sought-after Skills

There are a myriad of resources out there that offer guidance on how to go about picking up highly sought-after skills. While it's not possible to pick up *any* skill with ease, plenty of people less talented than you have developed skills or pursued a new profession that enables them to earn $100,000+ per year.

This is one of the best ways to scale a career quickly. There are a large number of jobs that can take you to the $50,000+ career mark without incurring the overhead costs of a four-year college education. Some examples of this that come to mind are:

- Contractor work (electrician, handyman, plumber, carpenter, welder)

- Software developer (websites, apps, etc.)

- Real estate agent or mortgage broker

There are many more examples of careers in fields like these where one can gain entry with less than one year of training and begin earning a higher than average salary. The great part about careers and skills like these is that there is usually an opportunity to do work on the side to make extra money. These types of skills might help the typical person accelerate toward early financial freedom more rapidly than say, becoming a lawyer or a doctor, where years of training and significant debts may be accrued.

The best part about many of these skills is that they might not require a full-time effort to acquire. You don't have to quit your job to become a software developer. You can learn for free or relatively low cost (compared to a college degree) through a number of different channels.

Clay did just that. In his mid-thirties, he switched from a career as a real estate agent's assistant to that of a software developer. After deciding to change careers, he attended a software programming boot camp for a few thousand dollars and worked hard for about nine months straight to become proficient as a web developer. He then applied, and was accepted to an internship at a real estate tech company. Clay, less than a year after deciding to switch careers, is now a full-time developer, and on a career track that offers him an excellent chance to command a six-figure salary within five years.

These types of skills require training and hard work, but in today's economy, more than ever, these skills are hired based on merit. All Clay had to do was prove he could do the work. Software engineers don't need to provide a degree! They are in high demand. They simply need to be able to demonstrate they can write code. Additionally, many software engineers find they are given perks, like flexibility with their hours and work location that directly enable them to make decisions unavailable to folks employed in more rigid positions.

If you aren't sure about your current career's prospects, developing a new, highly sought-after skill, and slowly building out credibility and demonstrable progress with it in the evenings and on weekends might be a great step in the right direction. After a few months to a year, you will know if this area holds your interest and you might be ready to switch over to the new career full-time, and then synergistically build up your own line of business on the side.

What skill you develop, and how you prove you have the qualifications to do the job will be up to you to tackle.

Step #2: Taking Control of One's Future Income

Most full-time salaried jobs offer security and consistency. Those performing well at a large corporation know where their next paycheck is coming from at all times, and know what their future looks like if they continue to do well. They are offered a picture of the best-case scenario right up front, and know where they will be in a few years, if things go well. The problem with this type of career is predictability. The fact that there is little to nothing you can do to change your income above and beyond the best-case scenario is the crippling drawback of salaried work. If your industry or career does not offer you the ability to take control of your income, you need to find a way to change—that is, if you want to move from an average income to an extraordinary one.

> *Ellie was working her first job at a Fortune 500 company as a financial analyst. She recalls the first time pay was brought up with her supervisor, about six months after she started. She was doing the same job as analysts with many years more experience, and expected this would be reflected in her performance evaluation. In other words, she thought that her pay would be based on merit. What a joke.*

> *She remembers sitting there and smiling politely as she received a 2 percent raise. She scored a 100—the highest possible score—on her talent assessment, volunteered for every assignment available, and went the extra mile to network with and get to know folks in every department of the company that she interacted with. She was even doing a bonus assignment that sought to save the company millions of dollars per year.*

> *Frankly, Ellie was bored. Work was too easy, and she wasn't being pushed. She had stopped learning, and had become aware she could literally handle all the work her entire team was doing, with time to spare. In other words, as far as she could tell, she was objectively among the very best at her role, in that company. And she was not getting rewarded for her effort or potential.*

Time for a stellar performance review, right? Nope. Ellie got a 2 percent raise. Maybe that's bad business from the company she worked for, and maybe that's not typical of how things work at other companies. But, rarely will one meet the person, who has a meteoric rise in a large or even medium-sized company to the point where they controllably go from making $50,000 to $100,000+ in two to three years without an objective change in their skillset or resume (for example, completion of an expensive MBA).

The problem for Ellie, and the problem for almost everyone in a corporate, salaried role is they aren't in control of their income. There is a limit to their potential, and there is someone else making judgment about their performance. Maybe she should have just shut up, taken her 2 percent, smiled, and got on with her spreadsheets, putting in her dues just like everyone else.

Maybe, she should have continued smiling politely, thanked her supervisor for her paltry raise, and been grateful to have the opportunity to continue earning a paycheck.

Instead, she faced the problem. She realized, of course, the blame lay with *her*. Not with the company, not with her supervisor, nor anyone in HR. *She* signed up for that tiny raise going in! She joined the company knowing their policy and her career track. She made the decision to sign up to play a game where the rules were clearly defined and the outcomes clearly spelled out. Sure, star networkers, performers, and those in the right place at the right time might be able to expedite progress to a slight degree. But, the fact of the matter is that no one at a large corporation goes from making less than $50,000 in a year to over $100,000 in just three to five years without changing something.

If Ellie had truly wanted to make real progress on the income front, she'd have signed up to play a different game. A game where the opportunity to earn is unlimited and where *performance* is directly tied to income. If you are a star (and you are), then what you want is objective pay. You want to either deliver against a metric and get paid, or fail and go home with empty pockets. Maybe that metric is sales, and maybe it's in retention of customers. Maybe it's in marketing, or maybe it's in finance and accounting. Regardless, you cannot scale your income without taking a position that rewards performance objectively and with infinite potential. This sounds well and dandy, right? Of course you would prefer to get paid for performance! The problem is that your boss would laugh at you if you asked him/her for that type of pay, right? Yes, even if you save the company $1M through your new initiative, your boss will laugh you out of a job if you ask her for 10 percent of those savings.

So, how do you go about getting performance-based pay? *The benefit to performance-based pay is that earnings can theoretically be unlimited.* There are many downsides, however. One downside is that those who do not deliver against their metrics receive little or no pay. Another disadvantage is that many commissioned salespersons, contractors, or similarly paid workers do not receive the cushy benefits packages offered by large corporations to their employees that earn large salaries. Finally, salespersons and commissioned consultants or contractors typically will have to spend months or even years developing expertise and a sales pipeline to begin producing results that can out-scale salaried income.

So, if you make a middle-class salary, and want the chance to earn performance-based pay, your mindset needs to be that this performance-based pay piece will come at the expense of your current salary, or that you will forgo a larger base salary. You will also have to accept that there will likely be an initial struggle where you may have to work harder, longer, and smarter than you are used to in order to outstrip the earnings of a cushy salaried job.

Okay, so let's stop here for a minute. This is the major point here. This is the whole argument of this section, this chapter, and this book, really. If you want to have a shot at earning way more money or at achieving financial freedom early in life, you will *likely have to give up a regular salary in a traditional career to attain it.*

This isn't always true—and there are plenty of examples of folks who earn big bucks on big salaries, or negotiate hefty salaries, *and* large potential bonuses. But, these folks tend to have had long careers with proven track records. They have produced results and built their reputation over many years. They are not in it for early financial freedom, but for professional satisfaction, power, and impact in their chosen industries. Obviously, folks earning well over $150,000 per year, might find it very difficult to replicate that level of income even with performance-based pay. This argument doesn't apply to them.

Use common sense. Will your career path deliver opportunities to soar past six figures in income over the next three to five years? If so, stay in it! You are in control of your income and have developed highly sought-after skills! A thrifty person who is house hacking and earning $150,000 per year will coast to early financial freedom in rapid time. That same person earning $50,000 will not.

If you want to have a shot at scaling your income and do not feel that the best-case scenario on your current career track will get you there, you need to change something. It can mean moving to a division in your company that does pay primarily for performance (like sales), it can mean moving to another company altogether. Remember, opportunities that come with truly scalable performance-based bonuses often come at the cost of a decrease in base salary. Do not interpret this by thinking you need to look for lower paying work. Instead, look for work that offers scalable income opportunities and accept that this may mean a reduction in base salary. You can do this because you have prepared by cushioning the short-term blow of lower salary with the cash you have stowed away early in your plan, and the passive income that flows to you.

As mentioned earlier, it takes sales professionals and consultants or contractors anywhere from a few months to a few years to develop a sales pipeline. So, there's high risk of a reduction in short-term pay when one goes from a high paying, salaried job to one that's performance-based. And, of course, there's a risk the new role won't pan out, and the envisioned income increase never materializes.

However, the risk of lower pay with performance-based pay needs to be weighed against the other, less obvious, risk. Remember Ellie, our financial analyst from earlier? Ellie *knows* she will under-earn, relative to her potential, if she follows the career track outlined by her company. She *knows* she will be an underpaid cubicle jockey by staying that course. Ellie *knows* that she will have to save her way to financial freedom, one month at a time, $1000 to $2000 at a time, over the better part of a decade, if she remains a cubicle jockey. That's a real risk too. Ellie needs to decide if she really is a rock star. Rock stars aren't "marketing analyst IIs."

The risk of slowly having your dreams crushed by working your tail off for 2 percent annual raises is very real as well, and likely more devastating than being broke for a year or two trying to make your way with performance-based work. But, if you have saved up that first $25,000 and can live for a year or two on savings alone, then all that doesn't matter. You can figure it out without fear of financial ruin. Those with that financial picture going in will be able to clearly understand that the risk of not living up to their potential is far scarier than the risk of losing a soul-sucking corporate gig.

Performance-based pay doesn't have to be a sales gig, although sales are perhaps the most common way to break into this field. You might be able to find work at companies that will pay you to scale certain key metrics, or that pay for producing certain specific results. But, however you achieve it, understand that the cost of performance-based pay will usually be a lower base salary in the short-term, and perhaps fewer benefits and cushy corporate perks as well.

Step #3: Find Synergies between One's work, Side Gigs, and Investments

Scaling your income can be the hardest thing you ever do, or it can be an automatic breeze. The difference between the two comes down to synergy. Synergy means doing two or more things that work together to produce a result greater than either activity on their own. Synergy means working on a project that's directly related to something else that you do anyway, like working on a house that you live in, working overtime, or applying your professional skills to freelance work at a high hourly rate, in a manner in which boosts both your skills and your success at your endeavors.

Too many people hear about folks who got rich by starting an online business in their basement after work and think that applies to them. Too many people hear about folks who flipped houses, began freelance consulting, started an ecommerce site, or myriad other business ideas. They hear about this and then go off and pursue their "passion" or an idea that appeals the most to them. Unfortunately, much of the time, this is not an effective way to move toward early financial freedom. Ellie, the financial analyst discussed earlier, would be foolish to try to build an ecommerce site selling modern art in her spare time. Starting a website has almost no overlap with corporate finance. If Ellie were a software engineer or web marketer, then a website business synergizes with her profession. Options that are good for Ellie include part-time bookkeeping gigs and part-time financial consulting for small businesses. They include work that directly uses her professional skillset and that give her the chance to gain more experience while earning large amounts of money per hour.

If you want to have a good shot at succeeding, choose to go down paths that are synergistic with your current life circumstances and career! While complete career turnarounds have happened successfully in the past, doesn't it make sense to use the professional skillsets and core competencies that you've built up as the foundation for your new jobs and business ventures? Obviously, if you detest your work or feel that there are no scalable opportunities for folks with resumes similar to yours, it may be time for a complete career reversal. But most people will be able to find opportunities that make tons of sense given their current professional experience and desired income!

Clay (our real estate guy turned software engineer) is a great example of this. Yes, Clay switched from a career as a real estate broker to one in software development. But, he works for a real estate investing website. This synergizes his new technical expertise with his long career in real estate. Clayton is uniquely qualified to do some of the work he does, and thinks through issues that other software developers who lack a real estate background might miss!

The worst thing you can do is try to have two totally separate jobs at the same time. This is a recipe for disaster for quickly giving up on your dreams. Instead, choose something synergistic with your ability to earn more.

Side Hustles

Many folks who write and teach about money management, as it pertains to early financial freedom, discuss the concept of having a "side hustle." When they use the term "side hustle" they are referring to the concept of starting a business or moonlighting (working a second job or freelancing). The goal is to grow that income stream to the point where it's capable of surpassing their lifestyle expenses or replacing the income from their W2 jobs.

Side hustles can work and there are tons of examples of this approach being used all over the world. However, side hustles should be thought of as an extra step. They are far less likely to have dramatic impact on one's financial position than making critical changes to how the workday is spent.

Passion VS Pay

"Follow your passion!" is a refrain heard time and again by young people in America. In this ideology, if you do what you love, the money will follow.

This is true for some, but not for most.

If your passion is software engineering, construction, or business analytics, by all means, follow your passion—the money will follow. If your passion is political science, art history, literature, video games, or similar, that's wonderful. However, you'd better be 100 percent committed and prepared for a very tough career ahead. You'd better be willing to dive in head-first and allow your passion to consume the better part of your waking hours. There's just too much competition and too little demand for jobs in some fields for them to be worthwhile. If you just happen to like history better than math, but don't find yourself reading late into the night with regards to your so-called passion, you should not pursue it with your career. You need to pursue something marketable instead. While millions of people find history enthralling, only hundreds or perhaps dozens of people find the analysis of the same event, person, or culture truly fulfilling.

Here's the good news: you will become financially free at an extraordinarily early age. You will have most of your life to pursue your passion(s) without having to worry about a paycheck. However, your income production will have to come from a scalable career. Similarly, if you have yet to discover your passion, stop trying to find it. Develop a skill or career in a well-paying field that works for the time being. I'll give you a hint—you'll learn to love almost *any* career that you become good at and for which you are rewarded handsomely.

Do not be a fool and think that the world will embrace your enthusiasm for marine biology or 18th century English history with a high paying career. Study those passions in your free time and enjoy them in early retirement from wage paying work. Pursue a career that is in more demand with your professional full-time efforts. This decision is made *in college* for millions of Americans. Don't go through a four-year degree and spend tens of thousands of dollars to educate yourself on a subject with little commercial value. Why bother going to college at all when you can learn for fun and for free on your own time? Instead, pursue a degree that places you at some advantage in the marketplace. Understand that degrees that are unlikely to provide value in the marketplace are a sunk cost—you will have to start from scratch and learn something truly profitable if you desire to earn more income.

Pursue your passion professionally if, and only if, it is marketable, or if you are willing to do whatever it takes to rise to the top. Otherwise, pursue a professional career that is in demand and scalable. Start over if you made the wrong choice, and accept the fact that your choice to pursue something that does not pay well was a decision that delays early financial freedom.

Why Do So Few People Take Control of Their Income?

Good people, smart people, professional people are paid for their efforts, and given a steady paycheck the world over. They receive a salary and a 2 to 4 percent annual raise with a promotion every couple of years if they show up on time, play nice with the boss, and dress and act appropriately during the workday. There is nothing wrong with that, and millions of folks like this contribute greatly to society. The fact of the matter, however, is that the vast majority of these folks are going to work a long career and retire with, at best, modest wealth late in life.

That's a recipe for a forty-year career, although it's still possible to retire far earlier than that with an extreme approach to cutting back on spending. But, people who are both frugal and proactive about scaling their income can achieve early financial freedom far faster. They might be able to go from few assets to permanent financial freedom in just ten years, or seven, or even five. It is the combination of high income and a strong savings rate that will truly expedite early financial freedom.

Those who don't want to go through the decades-long slog of saving a salaried paycheck and investing it in passively managed assets will need to change careers. The longer they wait to change jobs, the harder it will become, and the longer their road to financial freedom. Furthermore, the more specialized they become, the worse this problem will be as changing a career will mean wasting the years of their life spent gaining their specialized expertise. Instead, fundamentally understand the principles of success across many disciplines, and choose a few niches to focus on based on perceived opportunity.

But the hardest part is accepting the undeniable truth: If you are stuck in a white-collar job earning a middle-class salary, and aren't particularly passionate about your work, you *need to change jobs*. By this point, the logic behind this argument should be clear. But, you might be asking yourself the following question: "Why aren't more people doing this? Why am I surrounded with intelligent people with great degrees who work long hours and produce excellent work, who won't even consider the possibility of trying their hand at something different? They don't seem to particularly love their work, yet they aren't leaving. So why should I leave? Why should I do something that seems so extreme?"

The answer to this question might best be explained by an example.

Smart People Refusing to Collect Free Money

Ellie, our financial analyst, is a professional in the area of financial planning and analysis. She is able to look at the business of life (and the business of business) and crunch the numbers to determine where the most important and impactful changes can be made in business or personal financial models.

The vast majority of financial planners and analysts out there are equally or even more skilled than Ellie, working at large corporations, saving almost nothing, and working on almost meaningless models with negligible impact to their corporate or personal bottom lines. That, or they are crushing it in the investment-banking world, yet as a result of their chosen profession have no time to devote to the pursuit of financial freedom. In fact, the vast majority of Ellie's peers out there are attempting to maximize the returns of their stock portfolio, betting on giant corporations listed on the NASDAQ from their cubicles at work.

Ellie is determined not to become one of these people. She is determined to become financially free at an early age, and is willing to pursue opportunities that present themselves. Ellie is amazed that the MBAs she works with, people far smarter, far more skilled with a spreadsheet, far more technically knowledgeable about business than her, fail to manage their own wealth effectively. She is amazed they fail to miss the implications from a basic dataset (like their spending patterns) that reveals obviously important financial levers in their own lives. They can spot the myriad problems found in operating the business, but are unable to see those same flaws in their personal lives.

She works with MBAs who can build 1500 line spreadsheets, tying every expense out to the penny, and come up with beautiful projections for the future, yet fail to miss analysis on the very largest pieces of their own financial problems. These folks are the cream of the crop as far as business professionals go. However, they make rookie mistakes with their personal finances. While Ellie noticed this immediately, she thought these professionals must know something she didn't and gave them the benefit of the doubt. However, she quickly realized that, no, these financial professionals did not, in fact, understand basic personal finance or place any importance on wealth accumulation in their personal lives. The best example she can remember is the employee stock purchase plan.

Ellie's company offers a program that allows employees to purchase stock in the company at a 15 percent discount, vested immediately. What this means is that she can buy $100 in stock for $85, and then sell it for a $15 profit. She can do this for up to a specific sum each year (for instance, contribute $21,250 to buy $25,000 worth of company stock), and there are no penalties for doing so. In short, she had an opportunity to give herself a 15 percent profit, immediately.

The only catch? The money is put into a "fund" where it would sit throughout the quarter. The money would be withheld from her paycheck (she wasn't actually "buying the stock" throughout the quarter, just putting it into a fund, which purchased shares at the end of the quarter) and used to purchase company stock all at once at a set date. She could then turn around and sell the stock, the same day, and collect that 15 percent. Or, she could hang onto it, assuming she believed in the company's long-term prospects.

Ellie spotted this immediately, and immediately set out to buy the maximum amount possible as soon as she was eligible. She quickly found out something very surprising, however. Few of her coworkers were aware of this plan, and none of them were contributing a significant amount of money! *There must be some catch*, she thought to herself. However, after interviewing every single one of her highly educated and experienced colleagues, she realized there was no catch. The reason her colleagues didn't know about the plan was because they hadn't bothered to give it a look! They hadn't bothered to think about how to capitalize on their benefits and take advantage of an easy win.

Ellie decided to be a pioneer. She signed up for the plan, and received reduced paychecks for about fifteen weeks while the bulk of her paycheck went to the purchase of heavily discounted stock. Then, the quarter ended, she sold her shares, and pocketed a nice capital gain. She contributed about $5313 to the plan in the first quarter, and sold her shares for about $6250. In effect, she gave herself a $938 quarterly raise. Amazing. She had proved the system worked. This was a no brainer. Free money. All she had to do was survive for thirteen to fifteen weeks on a less-than-normal paycheck, and she collected this risk-free $938 gain.

She excitedly told her coworkers about her success, expecting a surge in signups for the plan. She even spelled out a thirty-minute procedure for her colleagues, including how to sign up for the plan, who to contact for questions, and an overview of how and why it worked.

But, none of them took her advice. Not a *single person* she showed it to took full advantage of the employee stock purchase plan. When she confronted her colleagues about why they would refuse free money, they had a lot of excuses.

Excuse #1: *"I can't live on a smaller paycheck for three months."*
Ellie had never considered this a problem, because she saved well over 50 percent of her income, and had accumulated a yearlong stockpile prior to taking part in the program.

Excuse #2: *"I'm afraid the stock price might fall when I go to sell it!"*
Ellie had considered the possibility the stock might crash in the two-hour period when she briefly held it. However, in all likelihood the stock would not increase or decrease in value by much in such a short time window, and even if it did, she felt she was just as likely to experience a gain as a loss.

Excuse #3: *"I can't be bothered."*
Ellie was baffled by this excuse. These were folks who spent the best parts of their day, during the best parts of their week, during the best years of their lives at their cubicles next to her. They spent their time jockeying for position in the corporate pecking order. They spent time building up their resumes line by line to make a case for their next promotion and raise. They went to business school and incurred tens or hundreds of thousands of dollars in debt to make themselves more marketable.

The process she had outlined took a total of thirty minutes to implement and would produce an immediate $3750 per year increase in income. How can they be so focused on their careers (spent managing finance), and so little on easy wins for the own personal wealth?

Excuse #4: "I'll have to pay taxes on the gain!"

Frustrated, Ellie shot back, "Yes, you will have to pay taxes on the gains. If you'd like, you can hand your next raise over to me. I will happily pay the taxes on that increased income, and pocket the remainder!"

This story really happened. These excuses really were used to decline a $3750 per year raise, and really were spouted by professionals with decades of experience and top-notch business educations. Even brilliant people fail to see that their job is what's holding them back, just as even brilliant people can miss easy wins that are right under their noses. These people were shown evidence of a benefit that could make a large difference in their finances with minimal effort. They had all the facts lined up, and the two-hour procedure to making thousands of extra dollars per year spelled out simply. Yet, they refused to take the obvious actions needed to advance their own interests.

Ellie quit that job soon after. She realized that the reason other people don't quit their jobs—even those with obviously lousy prospects—is the same reason they don't take advantage of the free money in the Employee Stock Purchase Plan. They are either scared to try something new, unable to handle even a temporary reduction in cash flow, or too lazy to bother to educate themselves. These problems afflict millions of people in this country. Folks who would otherwise rationally pursue financial independence and greater income opportunities hold themselves back and instead follow the herd.

The problem isn't that people are stupid. Ellie's coworkers were smart, hard-working people. The problem is that people who work really hard for money put almost no thought into managing it once they earn it. People don't manage their money because their peers and associates don't manage their money. It's not "normal" to try to live life intentionally, doing what you want, when you want to do it. It's not normal to stop all cash flow temporarily so that in three months you can buy $6250 worth of stock for $5313 and sell it immediately for a capital gain. It *is* normal to show up at work at eight, leave at five, complain about the new corporate policy that makes no sense, negotiate for a raise, and resume complaining about how you are underpaid. It's normal to buy yourself into a lifestyle that forces you to earn almost exactly the amount of money that you receive in your paycheck.

The folks Ellie worked with are people who can get every single detail correct on an exam, legal document, or business plan, yet have holes in their personal lives and budgets so glaring that a child could point them out. Some folks loved their jobs, and others didn't, but none of them had a plan in place to put themselves in a position where they were no longer dependent on their job within a reasonable period of time—like a decade or less. In fact, Ellie worked at a pay-TV company. Surely those working in that industry in 2017 would be wise to set themselves up for early financial freedom and remove dependence on income from a dying industry!

Ask any child the biggest pieces of the pie in Average Joe's spending and time usage? The analysis is obvious; for expenses, it's the housing and transportation sections, and for time, it's the work/career and sleep components. It's crystal clear. It's not hard. This isn't something millions of professionals are unable to recognize.

But better analysts than Ellie often fail to understand the basic, obvious takeaways from simple datasets. Better analysts than Ellie fail to piece together the data collected from hundreds of millions of American lives to see what works and what doesn't. And some of the best analysts in the world fail to see the obvious problem preventing them from escaping the rat race and living the life they choose, instead of one chosen by a middle manager.

Smart people utterly, bafflingly fail to see that their job/career is the reason they earn so little. And that it's the most important thing to change if they want to change their income! Don't be that brilliant professional who contributes greatly to an organization, yet buys himself into a lifestyle where he is incapable of pursuing any dreams beyond those of the next rung of the corporate ladder. Don't become dependent on a standardized career track with predictable earnings increases. Don't wake up in five years and realize you are underpaid. You know exactly what you are getting yourself into as a wage earner at a typical organization. There is no excuse for earning too little.

Don't Be Scared to Lose Benefits, and Understand Their Purpose

Healthcare, Life Insurance, 401(k) plans, vesting stock options, paid days off (PDO), and other perks are part of the deal when working at a large corporation or when earning wage income. Americans expect things like healthcare, insurance, 401(k)s, vesting stock options, PDO, and the rest of it. While these benefits obviously provide value, don't lose the forest for the trees. Benefits are nothing, *nothing*, in comparison to the opportunity to scale.

These benefits trick employees into thinking that a job is secure. Do not view them this way. Understand their purpose. Their purpose is to convince you to stay at a job as long as you are needed. They are offered to keep you complacent and chugging along producing profit for the company. They make it more expensive and difficult for you to switch jobs or pursue new opportunities.

Think about how many poor suckers are working Ellie's career path described above because they are too afraid to lose their health insurance, their 401(k) match, their unvested stock options, or their accrued paid time off! Benefits are *amazingly* effective at keeping great people in middling roles at companies for years and years. Many people don't like their jobs. When asked why they stay, they say things like, "I'm waiting for my promotion in March," or "In two more years I'll be fully-vested!" These folks are literally working a job they despise, for *years* in exchange for petty amounts of un-realized benefits or promises. Their benefits are often less than five figures in total value. That kind of compensation can be earned in a single sale in many industries. These bonus structures and scheduled promotion plans create a situation where things that are of tiny value are exchanged for the most valuable thing in life: time.

Don't be enslaved by benefits. Understand they pale in comparison to the ability to scale objectively against a metric, the ability to scale with the company's production, and the ability to work or not work on your terms. Do not ignore their value entirely—obviously benefits do have value, but understand that benefits should be distant considerations compared to perceived opportunity. Standard benefits aren't necessities that must be provided by your employer. You can buy your own insurance, save for medical expenses, and contribute to retirement accounts outside of your company's plan. Do not fall into the trap of believing that all is lost by giving up these benefits. Pursue opportunity, not stability. Stability is ensured by your continually lengthening financial runway, not by an employer's cushy benefits package.

Conclusion

It's really quite simple, you only have a few choices if you want to increase your income, and have no capital with which to invest in income-producing assets:

- Go out and develop a new skill that's worth hundreds of thousands of dollars per year.

- Get a job that rewards performance with unlimited upside.

- Start a business.

- Freelance or start a side hustle.

- Get creative and synergize your income-producing pursuits.

Of course, folks with little to no net worth, or just their first $25,000 or so in accumulated capital may find some of these paths more advantageous than others. Starting a business and freelancing on the side are relatively unlikely to produce material economic benefits when compared to having the ability to work all day toward increasing one's income. Of course, others have proven to be exceptions to this rule time and again—decide what is reasonable and likely to be effective for yourself.

Put yourself in financial position where you are unafraid to pursue opportunity. Put yourself in financial position where the cushy benefits of a dull job with little potential can't hold you back. Don't be one of the millions of smart, talented people who are too lazy, afraid, or financially incapable of challenging the status quo to pursue their dreams.

If you are determined to stay with your current job and try to earn more income in spite of the low probability of significant success, then at the very least pursue an opportunity that synergizes with what you are currently doing. But, you are far more likely to realize satisfaction and results with your workday by taking control of your income in the form of performance-based pay or other scalable opportunities. Understand that the cost of opportunity is very often a reduction in base pay, and that you will have to save up to free to you to take advantage of those kinds of opportunities. Part I comes before scaling your income for a reason. It is because those with a large stash of cash and low monthly spending can pursue opportunity with little risk.

Of course, if your chosen profession offers little opportunity to scale and little chance at synergistic, on-the-side income opportunities then you will have to swallow your pride and start over with a new one. That is, if you wish to have a chance at earning a high income in the near future. Choose more wisely this time, and pursue one of the many professions that offers a chance for freelance work, large income, and other opportunities.

Chapter 7
Scaling a Scalable Career

The last chapter should have made things abundantly clear: You cannot become wealthy quickly while working a full-time job and pursuing no outside income opportunities. Furthermore, while it's possible to earn significant income through a side business or by moonlighting, it's highly unlikely. A more effective plan is to make the changes necessary so you can pursue a scalable career that you're passionate about with the best part of your day, and to make that change as soon as possible.

This chapter discusses more general career advice. The advice here won't be a surprise, given some of the other things discussed earlier in the book, but the advice offered herein is important, and it's advice that's often ignored. Understand that you lessen your odds of success when you fail to do fundamentally important things right. Understand that the habits you've formed by becoming frugal and efficient with your lifestyle synergize with the goal of earning more money. The purpose of this chapter is to teach you some fundamentals that will help you to perform in scalable careers. These are fairly universal truths to business and career success, and are pretty straightforward.

If you have made the decision to move away from your dead-end career and into a profession that offers a real chance at upside in the short-medium term, now comes the fun part. You are now entering a world where results matter, not just showing up and doing what you are told. If you want to get ahead in this new world where performance is rewarded you are going to have to really perform, perhaps for the first time since you entered the workforce. Performing is different than showing up. Many wage-earners show up for work, do what they are told, and are paid for doing what they are told. Performance-based pay means you have to deliver results against a metric. Performance-based pay means you have to become creative and produce outsized results to earn outsized pay. What you do and how you do it matters more than for those who are paid a salary regardless of their performance. You are leaving the world of pass/fail that's salaried work, and entering the world where performance and pay are measured against an infinite continuum.

Five Tactics To Help You Earn More Money

1. Put yourself in a high achieving environment.
2. Read and self-educate forever.
3. Focus on continual improvement.
4. Instantly make trivial decisions.
5. Put yourself in position to get lucky.

Tactic #1: Put Yourself in a High-achieving Environment

Regardless of whether you choose to pursue a new high paying scalable skill, or choose to pursue performance-based pay, you will want to surround yourself with the very best people possible.

Potential is stifled when ambitious young stars go into a company where there is an entrenched hierarchy, and a set path for advancement. All one has to do is to remain on good terms with the boss, show up on time, put in a little "butt time" at their desk late into the evenings every now and then to show off with a few well-timed bursts of extra effort, and they will be promoted on a set schedule and advance through the ranks. While these might be fine people, former achievers with high intelligence, this kind of environment sucks out the soul. It kills ambition and destroys the hustle that's capable of helping folks have a truly great, rapidly advancing career.

Instead, put yourself in an environment where you are constantly surrounded by achievers who are performing at a far higher level than your peers at other companies. You need to find people who are truly great in your industry. My mentors are Josh Dorkin (Founder and CEO of my employer, BiggerPockets) and Brandon Turner (podcast cohost and a self-made real estate multimillionaire before age thirty). These guys are high achievers. I knew that before I joined them because I listened to their podcast, heard their story, and saw that they were building businesses and reputations in the industry that I wanted to be in. When the opportunity to work with them presented itself, I took full advantage, and have reaped the rewards in terms of accelerated learning, income opportunities, and chances to build my reputation.

This isn't to say that the people at a regular company aren't good people. It's simply to say that most people aren't in a position to produce at a high level, or to produce rapid and scalable results. Their achievements would simply move up a modest promotion and/or raise by a few months. While these people may make an impact over time, they will not be doubling or tripling their incomes in less than a decade, should they remain in their former positions. It's not because of their inability to perform; it's because of their environment.

In addition to the people you surround yourself with, think about the physical space and tools and equipment you have access to. Working in cramped conditions surrounded by folks who like to chitchat will not help you be productive. Instead, design a work environment that provides you the physical space and amenities that you need to be able to concentrate on important work for long periods of time.

Furthermore, you should have access to the tools you need to get the job done right. Do you work for someone who provides you with dated equipment and limits your access to commonly available resources like the Internet? Or, do you have state-of-the-art equipment and access to any and all information that you could want?

What is your environment at work? Are you surrounded by people who you admire, who you want to emulate and learn from? Do you have a wonderful physical workspace complete with state-of-the-art tools and equipment to help you get the job done right? You need to do everything in your power to surround yourself with an environment that will demand success from you. You can't afford not to if you want to truly get ahead in your career and have a chance to scale your income.

Tactic #2: Read and Self-educate Forever

Want to make more money and be more successful in your career? Pick out a business book from your local library and read it. Then, the next week, read another one. Repeat this forever. You might not have had a long career. But Dave Ramsey has. And he can share how he built a great company and hired/trained excellent producers in his book *Entreleadership*. You may not know how to produce exponential growth in your personal and professional life. But Darren Hardy knows. He wrote *The Compound Effect*, which shares the secrets to exponentially increasing one's capabilities. You may not know how to manage others. But Kenneth Blanchard, author of *The One Minute Manager*, does! Peter Drucker does. Jim Collins does. And they share huge chunks of their collective lifetimes of accumulated knowledge with anyone willing to read their books. The same is true for behavioral economics, investing, real estate, sales, organizational development, corporate strategy, brand building, customer service, and the like.

Does experience matter? Yes, and you will become a better producer with time and experience. But, you can't experience everything. No matter how much you've done personally, you have a lot to learn—and you can, from the best in the business. Choose to learn from the very best on a daily basis. Choose to continually self-improve with the fundamentals of personal productivity and leadership in your industry.

Business decisions are not difficult when the decision has been made by a brilliant mind before you and quite clearly applies to your situation. Or when you have the experience of five leaders to draw upon when working through a problem. Or when you are aware of dozens of problems that other companies or people like you experienced while completing similar projects. Or when you are aware of the simple steps needed to sidestep expensive issues when building out a new system that's already in place at dozens of other companies, but hasn't yet been built at yours, or implemented on your team.

Personal success authority Brian Tracy says the following: "One hour per day of study will put you at the top of your field within three years. Within five years you'll be a national authority. In seven years, you can be one of the best people in the world at what you do." A book a week roughly translates into about an hour of study a day. This is what it takes to attain an income in the top 1 percent of all Americans. (The threshold to be in the top 1 percent was $389,436 per year, according to an Economic Policy Institute Study in 2013.[1]) In other words, reading and taking to heart one book per week, fifty books per year, will make you one of the best-educated, smartest, most-capable, and highest-paid professionals in your field. Join the ranks of that upper echelon in the world of business over the course of the next few years, and do it for free or cheap through self-study.

The fact that you're reading this book is great. When you are finished,

---

[1] Sommeiller, Price, and Wazeter, *Income inequality in the U.S. by state, metropolitan area, and county* Online.

get out and read another, and another, and repeat for as long as you have a career that you are passionate about excelling in, or a goal that you believe is worth pursuing. This is so easy, so simple, and so obvious, that it is amazing more people don't do it.

By the way, while books are important, there are plenty of other ways to get equally good self-education. Things like podcasts, online courses, well-written blogs, and other online publications can provide educational opportunities just as powerful as books. It doesn't really matter how you go about learning from the best, so long as you make it a regular habit.

Tactic #3: Focus on Continual Improvement

In today's economy, it is no longer good enough to show up, work hard, go home, and call that an honest day's work. All over the country, honest, hardworking folks who have done this for years are finding themselves out of work, and up a creek without a paddle. It's safe to say that any skill you might develop today could well be obsolete in a few years. Therefore, your value isn't in your ability to use specific software, or to operate specific equipment, but in your ability to stay up to date with skills that are relevant today, and in your ability to develop new skills.

In today's economy, virtually every task that's routinely done by humans can and will be automated by either software or machinery. While that means nearly every job is at risk in this economy, it also means new opportunities are continually created. To avoid becoming obsolete, and to take advantage of the plethora of new opportunities, you need to constantly improve to remain a valuable member of the workforce, capable of commanding a continually increasing salary. If you don't improve, by working smart, continuously learning, and continuously experimenting, you could find yourself out of work before you know it.

In fact, as millions of people have recently discovered, continual improvement is needed just to keep a job. In this book, we seek early financial freedom and a large income that will speed up that objective. To increase your income you will have to improve. And you will have to improve rapidly and continuously. You'll have to read, learn, network, and experiment. You'll need to find new ways to automate your job and take on more responsibility as fast as you can. That's reality. That's what you need to accept.

Many people don't accept that. They will continue to be left behind by the economy, experience stagnant wage growth, and ultimately be laid off. They look around and find that their skillset is no longer marketable, and, depressingly, turn to worse and worse alternatives to their former manufac-turing and office jobs. They fail to recognize that their former high paying work isn't returning, and that the demand for new skills is higher than ever. Don't let that happen to you. Continually improve and adapt at a far more rapid pace than the rest of the workforce. Stay far ahead, and, if you want to scale your income, keep on making that gap wider and wider.

Tactic #4: Instantly Make Trivial Decisions

Meet Carmen. Carmen is a busy professional and an average twenty-something. In the evenings after work, Carmen relaxes by watching some TV or Netflix. She finds herself taking a lot of time changing the channel or browsing on Netflix trying to find some-thing to watch. Occasionally, she'll spend thirty to forty minutes browsing through the menu looking for a show that fits her mood on a given day.

Let's do some quick math. Thirty minutes per day times four nights a week is two full hours per week picking shows and movies. Furthermore, this delay may cause Carmen to stay up far later than she intended watching TV, as she started really getting into a show or movie later than if she had immediately found a suitable program. The end result is wasted time, less sleep, and an overall really bad end to a day and start to the next!

Carmen spends large amounts of time picking out an appro-priate outfit to wear to work. And she puts a lot of thought into what she's going to eat for lunch. One day, Carmen realizes just how much time she is wasting on these decisions. She realizes these types of decisions don't matter very much, and that she just needs to pick something reasonable quickly, and be satisfied with her choice. Carmen realizes she needs to learn to instantly make trivial decisions.

The vast majority of decisions that are made on a day-to-day basis are fairly trivial. Yet, sometimes these small decisions can take up a tremendous amount of time. When it comes to trivial decisions, what matters isn't neces-sarily making the best choice, but making one that's *good enough* and putting that decision behind you. Obviously, some clothing is fit for work, while other outfits aren't, some lunches are healthy and some are bad for us, and some TV shows stink, while others are fairly entertaining. While instantly making trivial decisions can free up personal time, it is perhaps even more important in the workplace and in business. A trivial decision doesn't have a lasting impact. A trivial decision will not significantly change your life for better or for worse. Do not waste time on trivial decisions.

Trivial decisions can be disguised as important decisions. For example, there might be two extremely good or extremely bad choices to choose between. Assuming you have all the information, and there are no alternative options to consider, it's often good practice to just bite the bullet and go with one of the two alternatives. If the decisions are really so close you can't seem to pick one over the other, then the differences are trivial. Some great examples of this are when you are trying to prioritize tasks. If you aren't sure whether it's more important to turn in your financial report or your sales projection, just pick one! Do it, then move on to the next task.

If you instantly make trivial decisions, you will free up an amazing amount of time in your day to be productive. It is the inability to make trivial decisions that leads most people to have extremely busy days, but get very little done.

Tactic #5: Put Yourself in Position to Get Lucky

What truly makes someone successful? Is it skill? Talent? Being in the right place at the right time? Actually, is it that "luck" is one of the most important traits?

Many successful people attribute their success at least partially to luck, to being blessed, or to having great fortune in one or many key parts of their lives or businesses. This makes sense. Key connections, funding, inspiration, and breakthroughs often come about by chance, rather than through the direct planning or efforts that we take to get there. In fact, luck is defined as "success or failure apparently brought about by chance rather than through one's own actions."

While you can't predict luck—and you can't predict whether any given event will have a positive, negative, or negligible impact on your life or business—you *can* improve your chances of getting lucky. You can do this in three ways:

1. Learn to recognize luck.

2. Put yourself in position to get lucky.

3. Give others the chance to make you lucky.

Step #1: Learn to Recognize Luck

How does one recognize luck? A stroke of good fortune isn't always readily obvious to the casual observer. In fact, it's possible that an opportunity that others could only dream of has been dangling in front of you your whole life—or is sitting right next to you. The problem with most people is they're unable to see how lucky they already are because they have no goals, no vision, no plan, and no dreams—at least none they can clearly articulate.

If you don't have a clear goal, then you will probably not be getting lucky, and the rest of this section will be of no help to you. Do you have a goal? A plan? A passion? If the answer is none of the above, then how on earth will you be able to tell when that key connection comes into your life, when that key event comes to your town, or when an opportunity with a key organization appears before you?

Meet Jason. Jason's goal is to increase the size and scale of his real estate portfolio and net worth and to build passive cash flow and wealth in the form of appreciating equity in real estate. He is willing to hustle for it, plan for it, and grab any opportunity he can to work toward his goal. Jason's stated goal means that every time he comes across other folks who invest real estate in his local market, he has a chance to get lucky. This would not be a fortunate event for most people; if someone else's goal was to be a big country music star, then a local real estate connection isn't a lucky meeting.

Jason meets key real estate connections in unexpected places— through his job in the tech world, while going for a run in the park, and even through social events. In fact, all three of those sources have proved absolutely critical in providing him with connections that help him succeed thus far in real estate. Jason is able to recognize luck and take advantage of these connections because he has a clearly defined goal, and wasn't afraid to talk with others in these organizations about his goal.

Most people wouldn't expect a chance meeting in a park or their social sports league to provide key connections, and Jason didn't either. Jason certainly had no intention of meeting investors during his workout or while playing pickup basketball. The point, however, is that these situations wouldn't have provided these lucky connections, if Jason didn't have the goal of investing and building a real estate business in the first place.

If Jason did not have that written, clear, dedicated goal set firmly in his head, a chance meeting with a real estate investor would not be a lucky event for him. Nothing would have come from those connections that would further his goal, and he'd be another unlucky schmuck. Jason is pretty lucky because he knows exactly what he wants with his career and real estate business. It makes spotting luck very easy for him.

If you don't have any goals and aren't sure what you want to do with your life, how on earth are you going to even know if you are getting lucky? You have no chance at good fortune because you don't even know what good fortune looks like!

Step #2: Put Yourself in a Position to Get Lucky

You will not be getting lucky if you spend the majority of your time behind a dusty cubicle, commuting in a car, and in your own home or apartment wasting time watching TV or playing video games. Luck presents itself to those who put themselves in position to take advantage of it. While luck can strike anywhere at any time, you can increase the chances of becoming lucky by physically or virtually putting yourself in front of people and opportunities.

Jenna considers herself a lucky girl. However, she has yet to make a lucky connection or gain a bit of inspiration whilst watching Netflix or TV or while playing video games. It seems that hanging out in your apartment/house by yourself, not working toward a goal is a behavior that's unlikely to produce a lucky outcome.

Instead, most of Jenna's luck comes when she spends her leisure and free time meeting face-to-face with people, having conversations with strangers, attending events, and joining organizations that she is passionate about. When she positions herself out in the world with at least the chance of meeting other people, when other people are at least around, that's when she makes lucky connections. Jenna is luckier than average though. Why? Because she goes a step further, and puts herself in positions where she is around very targeted people who can help her with her goals.

Jenna meets many key connections by spending time at networking events, meeting with local friends who share her goals and interests, and even spends her time online interacting with people in her industry on popular websites. On the other hand, Jenna makes fewer such connections at the bar at 1:00 a.m. or while watching Say Yes to the Dress. *Shocking, right?*

You will not become lucky by sitting at your cubicle and eating a sandwich at your desk. You may, however, become lucky during that same lunch by meeting someone who has done what you are trying to do and picking their brain. You will not get lucky playing *League of Legends* on your computer. You might get lucky by attending a local meet-up of folks aspiring to attain financial freedom. Of course, positioning yourself to get lucky is only possible if you have mastered step one above, defined your goals, and have the ability to both recognize luck and put yourself in a position where the odds of having positive chance events occur are excellent.

Step #3: Give Others the Chance to Make You Lucky

Remember Jason from the first step? The guy interested in building a real estate portfolio? Jason tells everyone he knows he is looking to build his real estate portfolio and wants to learn as much as possible. He talks about it at real estate networking events, to friends, to family, and to random strangers he meets while out and about. He even discusses it with people who aren't even remotely close to being in a position to buy real estate or help him with buying real estate.

Is this annoying? Probably. But it also brings him opportunity.

Jason has met multimillionaire real estate investors who are connected to him in unexpected ways because of his tendency to tell others about his goals early and often in conversation. One investor in particular gave him some incredible advice, which he was able to apply immediately to his investing strategy. This included access to information he hadn't previously thought to take advantage of to gain a clearer grasp on local market conditions—and even some insight into the state of the local commercial real estate market.

Jason is extremely lucky to be able to pick this investor's brain when facing big, strategic decisions. If Jason didn't tell anyone about his professional and real estate goals and kept his cards close to his chest, that opportunity and others like it might never have materialized. Jason might never have become financially free through real estate, and might still be working his day job hoping for his lucky break. In other words, he'd be out of luck.

Many smart people believe that telling the world what you're doing, spilling your secrets, sharing numbers, and telling others about your best practices is a *bad* plan. They believe this because they think it encourages competition and allows others to copy, mimic, and take away their patented systems.

Sure, it's possible some of the folks Jason talks to might compete with him for properties he would want to buy. That's perhaps even likely, as he meets more and more people in his industry. However, the opportunities and perspectives he develops will likely far outweigh the occasional times where folks take advantage of him.

Keeping goals and plans closely held may be beneficial in the short-run in specific cases. But, over the long run, the guy who makes known his intentions to the world and is constantly seeking aid in his pursuits will experience infinitely more luck. Don't let the fear of others taking advantage of you get in the way of the many, many more folks out there who are happy, willing, and able to help you achieve your goals.

So, are you lucky?

Conclusion

It's possible to go from $25,000 to $100,000 or more in net worth through savings alone, while working a full-time salaried job, and while renting an apartment. But, it's a slow process. This book is about early financial freedom. It's about building a life changing state of wealth as rapidly as possible. It's about putting yourself in position to take advantage of real opportunities and make big changes.

If you want to speedily achieve early financial freedom, you will want to turn your housing into an income-producing asset. You will want to save as much money as you possibly can. You will also want to start earning more money. The traditional corporate ladder is unacceptably slow for those looking to achieve early financial freedom and must be discarded. Instead, a new skill must be developed, one must learn to accept performance-based pay, and one must learn to synergize their professional skillsets with creative pursuits to help them earn additional income.

If you are serious about your career and increasing your income potential, you will need to push yourself. Surround yourself with a high achieving environment—both physically and with people that push you and bring out the best in you. Study hard through self-education on carefully selected topics, and take the materials to heart. Apply your education continuously and eagerly seek out opportunities to learn new skills and take advantage of new opportunities. In today's economy, skills are becoming rapidly obsolete.

He or she who adapts and learns quickly will always have work, and with increasing income potential. Do not belabor trivial decisions. Make them quickly and spend your time and energy on high impact tasks that require your concentration. And, make sure that you put yourself in position to get lucky. The harder and smarter you work, the luckier you'll get.

These steps are powerful ones, with the potential to dramatically speed up the accumulation of net worth.

Part III
Moving from $100,000
to Financial Freedom

In part I, we described how to accumulate your first $25,000 by living frugally, and explained how this helps springboard you toward opportunities to reduce or eliminate your housing expenses and increase your income potential. In part II, we used that first $25,000 and its year of financial runway to purchase housing and transition into work that offers greater potential on the income front.

When you have succeeded at part II, the ball really begins rolling. At this point, you live a low-cost lifestyle. At this point, you feel confident taking chances with new job opportunities. At this point you know how to live for free or for exceedingly low cost. At this point, you are accumulating thousands of dollars in cash per month from your high-income job and frugal lifestyle, and have accumulated tens of thousands of dollars in easily accessible wealth. Your assets are likely to rapidly expedite financial freedom, and your progress is accelerating. You are going to be hard to slow down.

Now it's time to use that accumulated wealth to create passive income. It's time to learn how to invest in such a way that you are never again dependent on wage income to pay for your lifestyle, so that you are *Set for Life*.

Chapter 8
An Exploration of Financial Freedom

Thus far, we have discussed saving money and earning money. Thus far we have discussed accumulating readily accessible cash. And you are now building an impressive nest egg. You now are transitioning from little to nothing, to moderately well off. It's time now to learn about building real, lasting wealth. Let me introduce you to the concept of wealth, why it's important to both you and to society as a whole, and how *wealth* differs from *income*.

There's this perception that rich people have some kind of unfair advantage over the rest of us. There's this feeling that they must be doing something underhanded to accumulate millions of dollars, when most people have so little. There's this emotional reaction that something isn't right in the world when it comes to the distribution of wealth and income.

"Fair" is all about individual perception, and only results when folks compare themselves to others in relatively similar positions. Folks will become incensed upon learning that someone they perceive as less qualified or experienced gets promoted ahead of them at work, yet have no trouble accepting the fact that entertainers like Kim Kardashian make millions of dollars per year.

The point of this part of the book is to give you the knowledge to produce an unfair financial result—unfair relative to your peers. This may put you in the position of being able to pursue your interests without distraction, without the need for work. This is about as unfair advantage as it's possible to attain. As soon as you perceive that, as soon as you stop whining about the unfair disadvantages you have specific to your case, your life, your job, or your family, the sooner you can begin pursuing this "unfair" opportunity to become truly free, in this period of great opportunity.

Human beings are inherently different in many ways. We differ first and most obviously in our physical strength, stamina, height, and weight—our physicality. We are also different in our ability to think, reason, and judge—our mental prowess. Finally, we differ in our outlook, work ethic, and humor—our attitude. It's an uncomfortable realization—but an important one—to understand that if the above are true, then, as a matter of fact, some human beings are better or worse than others in each of these area. Perhaps we can even acknowledge that some individuals are far better than us in some or even all those areas.

Future NFL hall of famer Calvin Johnson and the average person differ rather dramatically in athletic prowess. The average person would expect to lose in everything from a sprint, to the high jump, to long distance running, to the balance beam, and any other competition imaginable. Extrapolating out Calvin Johnson's 4.35 forty-yard dash time at the NFL combine, we can reasonably assume that he would run a 100-meter-sprint in just about ten seconds. I run the 100-meter-sprint in 13.2 seconds. That's a huge difference, insurmountable in a lot of ways, but if we were to measure that mathematically, Calvin Johnson is about 30 percent faster than me. Along the same lines, I can just barely reach the rim of a basketball hoop ten feet off the ground. At the combine, Calvin Johnson reached a point that's over twelve feet, five inches off the ground. Mathematically speaking, he jumps 25 percent higher.

The point is that against Calvin Johnson, I, as an average athlete, would lose in every athletic competition I can dream up at the present. I'd also like to point out that in spite of the fact I'd lose every competition, the physical differences, between an average guy like myself and one of the greatest athletes of all time, are not that big. He's only perhaps 30 percent better. *But at the height of his career, his income was 20,000 percent higher than I earned at that point.* Is that unfair?

Regardless of whether this is fair or not, we must acknowledge the simple truth that *small differences in ability can result in massive income differences.* Calvin Johnson's athletic prowess earned him a $64 million guaranteed contract in his early twenties. In contrast, my skillset as a spreadsheet junkie out of college was worth about $50,000 per year, with no guarantees. In this case, the 30 percent variation in our physical ability amounts to a 20,000 percent income discrepancy—a guy like Calvin Johnson will make around 200 times what someone with my skillset makes in his early twenties.

When it comes to income, folks who produce better work can and should get better pay. Calvin Johnson, while in the league, produced excellent results. He was an excellent producer and was paid well as a result. This discrepancy might be considered unfair if income really made a linear difference in quality of life. There is no circumstance in which an average athlete would be able to physically compete with elite athletes like Calvin Johnson. Thus, it would be frustratingly unfair that his relatively small physical advantages (approximately 30 percent superior to my own) equates to an earnings difference that creates a lifestyle 200 times better than average.

But this leads to another question: Just how much does income matter when it comes to quality of life. Quality of life is, after all, what we really care about here, right? It is quite unlikely that quality of life is linearly impacted by income. A person with high earnings might drive a Lamborghini to work, whereas an average one might own a Toyota Corolla. Sure, the difference in cost between the vehicles is vast, but the quality of life difference is probably not that significant. While it's much more fun to drive a $200,000 car, it would be absurd to say that it is ten times better than driving a $20,000 Corolla. While there will be a spectrum of preference on this and other similar expenses, people will adapt to their surroundings and accept them as the norm within a matter of weeks. The, "This is so cool, I'm driving a fancy sports car!" feeling would almost certainly wear off after a month or so.

The reason that the energy and excitement from a material possession such as a car, home, or TV wears off quickly is due to a concept called hedonic (happiness) adaptation. Human beings tend to quickly become accustomed to changes—good or bad—and within a few weeks fall back to a level of happiness unchanged from prior to the change. For example, in a 1978 study called "Lottery Winners and Accident Victims: Is Happiness Relative?" the authors studied the happiness levels of lottery winners and paraplegics relative to a control group.[1] Both the lottery winners and the paraplegics reported similar levels of happiness, perhaps counter-intuitively. Human beings are amazingly bad at predicting the things that will make them happy with a high degree of accuracy.

The high earner might live in a huge house with fancy furniture and a huge TV. The below average earner might live in a space that's less than 700 square feet with a roommate. But, is watching *Game of Thrones* really that much better for the guy with the fancy stuff? How much more comfortable is his couch, bed, hot tub, or bathroom? What is the difference between having those luxuries as a big spender and making it as your regular Joe?

---

[1] Brickman, Coates, and Janoff-Bulman, *Lottery winners and accident victims: Is happiness relative?*, 917–927.

The high earner probably eats at fancy restaurants or might even have a personal chef preparing his meals. A low earner might cook their own food and eat out at cheaper places. It would be very surprising if anyone making a median salary could not eat food that's very nearly as healthy and delicious as that consumed by the wealthiest folks on the planet. No, they might not eat lobster or caviar, but even relatively low earners can afford to purchase and prepare vegetables, fruits, and decent quality meats.

Income inequality doesn't really make much of a difference at the end of the day. Slightly better items and luxuries don't change the day-to-day freedoms and passions that individuals pursue. Life isn't 100 times better for someone earning $5M per year, versus someone earning $50,000 per year. Think about two different people: The guy who earns less than $25,000 per year but works twenty hours per week and surfs all day at a beach in Mexico, and the $1M-per-year executive who works seventy hour weeks. Who is happier?

The answer is that they're probably both happy in their own ways. One may love freedom; the other may love productivity/impact. They might also be unhappy—one might yearn for spending and luxuries beyond his means, while the other may yearn for the peace and quiet of the beach. So, if income inequality isn't that big of a factor in our happiness, what is the "unfair" part? What's the problem here? The primary problem is not that the elite athlete Calvin Johnson earns 200 times more than a regular earner. That's *income inequality*. The problem is in *wealth inequality*.

Income inequality is evidenced by pop stars, entertainers, and athletes reaching millions and being paid millions as a result. Wealth inequality might best be evidenced by Stewart Horejsi—an average guy you've probably never heard of who became a billionaire by buying stock in Warren Buffet's Berkshire Hathaway back in the 1980s. One person arguably produces a benefit to millions of people in our society. The other guy invested and just let his wealth grow for decades.

Jay Z (worth $552 million) and Dr. Dre (worth $700 million) are examples of famous people who have *wealth*. While they earned *high incomes* during their musical careers, it's important to distinguish their financial positions from those of Mike Tyson (bankrupted in 2003) and 50 Cent (declared bankruptcy in 2015).

Tyson and 50 Cent are examples of high-income earners who managed to accumulate little *wealth*. They both went bankrupt, and it's important to remember that's about the same amount of assets as the person begging on the street corner. While they will probably go out and earn more down the line, their ability to control their environment will be limited to what others pay them, unless they learn to build wealth. Jay Z and Dr. Dre will be wealthy forever, even if they never produce another piece of music.

Where income inequality becomes a real problem is when it's combined with wealth inequality. Income is usually (but not always) based on merit and natural ability. Income can be taken away and can come and go. Wealth, on the other hand, is a function of knowledge and time. Wealth in the right hands is much harder to lose, and in many cases, increases forever.

Mike Tyson earning and spending hundreds of millions of dollars isn't a sign of systemic unfairness in society today. His power is likely limited to what he can collect during the most physically capable years of his life. It's actually the folks like Warren Buffet and Carlos Slim (two of the wealthiest people on the planet), folks who have 1.5 *million* times more wealth than your regular American, that are the real outliers. Their wealth and power are virtually unlimited and perpetually growing. Furthermore, that wealth and power can be passed to the next generation and allowed to continue increasing infinitely.

Warren Buffet was worth $64,900,000,000 in 2016. Average Joe is worth $45,000. Average Joe is slowing down; Buffet is accelerating. *That's* the issue we are concerned with. But, is it unfair? Individuals like Calvin Johnson earn strong incomes early in their careers due to inarguable natural abilities—mentally, physically, or with respect to their attitudes and their work ethic. That part makes sense to most of us.

What's incomprehensible to many folks is that while the mega-rich billionaires of the world earn way more than Average Joe, they also understand how to make their wealth work for them. This is a manipulation of a wealth system that harnesses mathematical principles to snowball wealth over long periods of time into staggering sums.

Now, neither Buffet, Slim, nor any of the other billionaires or wealthy folks and high earners just discussed necessarily did anything wrong, and in many cases they have provided a lot of value to the world. But our society falls short when the masses neglect to become aware of the fundamentals of wealth creation. This knowledge and the skill of patience and long-term thinking are learned and must be taught early. When that fails to happen, the wealthy continue to snowball into ever more powerful, almost mythical beings, while much of society doesn't even know where to begin.

This part of the book will teach you about the incredible power of long-term wealth creation and principles of investing and value creation. It's about making your wealth work for you. And, it's about doing this in such a way so that you can make use of that progress in making life decisions today, not in thirty years when you might be too old to undertake the things you want in life. If you fail to understand these principles, you'll be stuck in a rut, likely complaining about rising income inequality and not understanding the real issue: *wealth inequality*. This is the fate of millions of Americans who are unable to accumulate wealth, in spite of living in one of the richest and most well paid civilizations in human history.

This is immensely important to our society, and my fascination with it—and fear of becoming one of the millions left behind—is why I have studied this subject so intensively, built personal *wealth*, and why I wrote this book. The early possession of wealth-building knowledge is an unfair advantage and the only way to level the playing field is to educate folks, early in their lives, on how to be successful given the current framework.

In chapter 6, we discussed learning how to earn more income. But it gets better than just earning more income. If you follow the process in this part of the book, you will build lasting wealth, the ultimate goal in finance. Wealth will allow you to live life on terms *you* dictate, beholden to no boss, client, or job. In just a few years of applied effort, you can set yourself up for life.

Who Are the Financially Free?

Let me introduce you to three people who are set for life:

> *Melinda is thirty-eight years old. She and her husband Camden have bought and sold five family homes in the past ten years. Each home needed extensive repairs, and the two tackled those projects with a do-it-yourself style. Between their jobs and the profit from selling these homes, Melinda and Camden have accumulated well over a million dollars, which they invest in index funds. The two of them now live off the dividend income from their funds. Melinda never misses her daughter's Girl Scout meetings, school plays, or sporting events. Melinda laughs at people who ask her to be somewhere before 8:00 a.m. Melinda works every now and then as a real estate agent when she is bored, and continues to fix up a new home every couple of years.*

Brady is thirty-three years old. He used to work at a bank but hated his job. Brady bought a cheap home at the age of twenty-one and fixed it up. He then rented out the extra bedrooms to his friends while he slept in the attic, so that he could live for free. Ten years later Brady finds himself a millionaire with dozens of rental properties. Brady spends his days starting businesses at a whim, writing books, playing video games, and traveling around the country, to the Caribbean, and to foreign countries.

Jonathan is forty years old. He built an online business that he started in his basement. It took him ten years to grow the business to a point where it could reliably provide for his family. Jonathan poured countless hours into the business and suffered large personal costs in the process. Today, Jonathan's business produces millions of dollars per year in income, and helps millions of people improve their lives. Jonathan does what he wants, hangs out with other multimillionaires, major political figures, and other leaders in the community. His business is so profitable he has a staff of over twenty-five people to run it for him. He stops by once or twice a week with donuts for his team, and spends his weekdays skiing with his daughters.

Each of these individuals earned income and converted it into wealth, or built a business asset that produces reliable income. Each of them put in years of frugality, hard work, sweat, and likely some tears, yet each of them now find themselves in the privileged situation of having their financial needs met without the need for anything close to full-time work. Each of them has achieved financial freedom.

What Is Financial Freedom?

Financial freedom is a state in which one has enough income from return on assets that they no longer need wage paying work to permanently sustain their lifestyle. There are an infinite number of ways to achieve financial freedom, but the principle always remains the same. The financial freedom equation is as follows:

Assets × Return > Lifestyle

Where "Assets x Return" is equal to the usable cash flow (in dollars per month) generated by your assets and "Lifestyle" is equal to your cost of living per month.

Once assets generate returns in excess of the spending needed to fund your lifestyle, then the financial freedom equation is satisfied.

Why Pursue Financial Freedom?

Financial freedom delivers exactly what it implies—freedom. Those who attain financial freedom are beholden to no job, boss, or company. They are free to choose how they direct their day in its entirety, without the need to generate income. They are free to live life as it was meant to be lived.

In this part of the book, the goal is to replace wage income with passive income. Wealth and passive income are not to be pursued simply for the luxuries that they afford. No, in this book wealth is respected first and foremost for its ability to buy choice. The folks in the examples above have already achieved financial freedom and have near total discretion to live their lives without the need for work.

Total freedom is the ultimate goal. But, freedom is a continuum. It will take many years for most readers to achieve true financial freedom. But, it takes considerably less time to achieve the freedom attained in parts I and II of this book. The benefits to accumulating wealth in those initial stages should be obvious, and the opportunities available will exponentially multiply for the individual as wealth is accumulated. Early financial freedom is the ultimate goal. But, financial *progress* continuously delivers more and more freedom as progress is made. One doesn't have to live like a hermit, spending little to nothing, steadfastly pursuing financial freedom. Instead, producing cash flow, accumulating large liquid reserves, cutting back on expenses, and increasing income can produce incredible benefits immediately.

Focus first on rapid financial *progress*, and you will notice gradual but incredible changes in the number of opportunities and freedoms that become available to you. The benefits of saving the first $25,000 are made clear in part I. The first $100,000 in net worth and four to five years in financial runway discussed in part II will produce correspondingly greater benefits.

The best way to demonstrate the impact of financial progress might be through a discussion of the four levels of finance. These four levels of finance range from the truly broke to the independently wealthy. At each progressively higher level, witness the drastic change in the amount of choice available to the individual. Those on the lower levels have substantially less freedom and ability to direct what they do with their time than those who have climbed to higher levels. While it is safe to say that money isn't necessarily a source of happiness, those who build wealth and attain financial freedom generally have more choices in life and more opportunities to seek that happiness than those who do not.

The Four Levels of Finance

Level #1: Cash Flow Negative

Level of Freedom: Lowest

A cash flow negative life is one in which an individual or family spends more than they earn. The vast majority of folks who are cash flow negative have a net worth very close to zero. In some cases, people leading cash flow negative lives can accumulate substantially negative net worth, but creditors learn quickly, and future access to borrowing becomes nearly impossible.

Cash flow negative lives have a bleak outlook. Long term, the consequence of a cash flow negative life is quite severe; in most cases the cash flow negative individual will lose much of the control over how they spend their time. Of course, many young people are cash flow negative, and would not be able to sustain their lifestyles without financial support from their parents or loved ones. Think of college students and adult children who live at home or have their rent subsidized.

> *Ashley is a schoolteacher with expensive tastes. With her low income and high spending, she is unable to pay for her rent on her own, so Ashley lives with her mom and dad. While her loving parents have and will likely continue to support her financially, this subsidy comes at a cost. Ashley isn't allowed to sleep over at her boyfriend's house. Ashley gets questions when she is out too late. Ashley never hosts friends. In fact, the only time Ashley's friends visited her house was when her parents had a yard sale! In case you are wondering, Ashley is twenty-seven years old. These constraints on Ashley's freedom are direct results of a cash flow negative life.*

In cash flow negative situations that do not involve these types of subsidies, there is the simple misery of constant and seemingly unending financial pressure. Debt payments, upcoming expense (anticipated and unexpected), and inability to build wealth or pursue opportunities make it nearly impossible to escape this trap.

Cash flow negative lives will need to work hard to get to neutral before they can begin pursuing early financial freedom. The good news is that many folks at this level can see a dramatic improvement in their lives, including measurable progress, with just a few months of concentrated effort.

Level #2: Cash Flow Neutral

Level of Freedom: Modest

Long term, a cash flow neutral life is one that's reliant on either a paycheck, or in the case of the self-employed, a small set of customers. Large life decisions are heavily dependent on the whims of a boss or are based on the changes and limited opportunities in one's chosen field.

Today, many nine-to-five employees are in this position and will be for the majority of their lives. A cash flow neutral life may be one that's increasing in net worth, but that accumulation is the result of some "default" settings accepted as normal in American life. Mortgage payments and the resulting increase in home equity, automated 401(k) contributions, and perhaps a handful of depreciating assets, like a couple of cars are the only significant contributors to net worth. All, or materially all, other dollars that enter the individual's life are spent accumulating luxuries of no lasting value.

The cash flow neutral category includes all lives that routinely save less than 15 percent of their total take-home pay. Mortgage payments and home equity do not count as savings, nor do retirement account contributions, since these assets are not usable in the short-term and do not generate usable cash flow. Imperceptible positive cash flow, or savings that are not accessible in the short-term, have no or tiny impact on financial decision-making power.

Note: Retirement accounts are discussed in the appendix, but please note for now that the reason that retirement accounts have so little impact on your financial position is in your perception of their usefulness. If you do not intend to harness that money until you're sixty-five, and are not near traditional retirement age, then it has no impact on your present ability to make decisions, and thus doesn't count as usable wealth in pursuit of early financial freedom.

The cash flow neutral individual will typically work long hours over a career lasting the better part of a lifetime, perhaps on the order of forty years or so. Cash flow neutral folks are often uneasy about their family's financial security and are thus uncomfortable thinking about or talking about money. They may also be uncomfortable with risks because anything that could potentially result in the loss of a job, major client, or career could result in a loss of cash flow, rendering them immediately cash flow negative.

Most often, folks with cash flow neutral lives believe they are doing the right things with their money. They see themselves as on track with their peers at work or neighbors down the block. It can be hard to convince these types of people that they need to rethink their financial position.

Asking a cash flow neutral person to repeat the following phrase tends to be an effective means of lighting a fire in their belly: *"The best possible outcome in my life, should I continue with my current career and savings rate, is that I end up in my VP's office over there (or one very much like it) doing his job, and doing it all day long every day of the week."*

If you are cash flow neutral and happy or enthusiastic about that phrase, then no further action is necessary, and you may find yourself unenthusiastic about the strategies in this book. Often, however, after just one repetition, it becomes relatively easy to encourage folks to begin taking simple steps toward moving up to a higher level. If you are cash flow neutral and want to change that, then start with part I of this book.

Level #3: Cash Flow Positive

Level of Freedom: High

Cash flow positive folks live well below their means and accumulate assets at a high rate relative to their earned income. These folks are able to work jobs of their choosing and are able to make major life decisions with thought given to their overall well-being first. They also have sufficient leeway in their lives to take risks with their careers and passions, should opportunity come a-knocking.

The difference between a cash flow neutral person and a cash flow positive person can be hard to spot. The cash flow positive individual might work the same job, wear the same clothes, and do the same things for fun, but there will be subtle differences. A cash flow positive person might not be seen with fancy new cars, eating out for lunch every day, or living in a lavish apartment. Over time, however, these folks will be starting businesses, acquiring property, making connections, or will otherwise be presented with opportunities that cash flow neutral folks are never exposed to.

Cash flow positive lives result in ever-decreasing dependence on others and lower tolerance for boring/ineffective work. They desire and seek out rewarding and engaging challenges in life.

Assisting these folks is fun and engaging—they actively want to improve

131

their own lives and often seek the counsel of others. The best way to assist them in improving their financial positions is to point them toward education, resources, and opportunities that will allow them to deploy their hard-earned savings for a good investment return. This will help them expand on the virtuous cycle that is earn, save, and invest, and continue to increase the freedom in their lives.

The four chapters in part II of this book should put you deep into cash flow positive territory.

Level #4: Financially Free

Level of Freedom: Highest

Financial Freedom is achieved when cash flow that requires no work (or minimal active work) safely and consistently surpasses total lifestyle expenses. It seems like a lot of folks fantasize that financially free individuals lead a life of leisure. They'll envision a nice beach, frequent traveling, massages, and other luxuries. While some folks do treat themselves to these types of lavish lifestyles, as a practical matter, the financially free folks are often some of the hardest workers and most frugal people around.

The reason these people work so hard is because they no longer need to work for money. They work to solve a problem they are passionate about, master a hobby they enjoy, or to build a business empire that will last for multiple lifetimes. Because they have total control over how they spend their time, they only participate in projects that are truly interesting and engaging to them. This part of the book will move you toward early financial freedom.

Wrapping Up the Four Levels of Freedom

Which level do you want to be at? How much freedom do you want in your day? Would you like to be able to do the following:

- Choose exactly where you live, what you eat, and how you transport yourself?

- Choose what job to work, not on the basis of salary, but based on the work itself?

- Choose whether to work *at all*, or to work on a schedule that better fits your moods?

- Build your own business one day?

- Be able to tell others to buzz off when they want you to wake up at a certain time, wear certain clothing, or perform uncomfortable or boring work?

If so, then you need to figure out a plan to get there. This part of the book provides that plan—a plan that will take you on an effective, steady, easy, virtually *automatic* path from level three to level four.

How to Go About Pursuing Financial Freedom

Financial freedom is attained when one no longer needs to work for money, and is achieved when the financial freedom equation is satisfied. The equation, again, is:

Assets × Return > Lifestyle

Note that this is a mathematical expression involving three parameters. Since an equation must be solved, we can see that finance is largely a math-based sport. This is great news, because each of the three parameters of the financial independence equation can be optimized and measured. It's possible to purchase income-producing assets by earning money and then saving it. It's possible to study investing and seek opportunities to earn outsized returns. It's possible to create or build assets that generate income. And, it's possible to cut back on lifestyle expenditures to reduce the number of assets and/or returns needed to sustain financial freedom! You should be doing all of those things to tip the balance of this equation in your favor. At the same time.

Part I focused on lifestyle design. Part II blended in income generation and housing. Part III will introduce you to asset acquisition and return on investments. These concepts were intentionally introduced in that order. At each stage of wealth accumulation, different parts of the equation are the most significant levers in wealth generation. However, you should be reading ahead. You should be thinking ahead. You should understand that wealth building isn't some rigid formula that's followed precisely. It's important to keep an investing strategy in mind, even when one has less than $10,000 in assets, just as it's important to stay relatively frugal even when one builds over $1 million in net worth.

Those who focus on each of these areas, constantly seeking out ways to improve all stages of their financial journey, will more rapidly attain financial freedom. Remember, the goal is to solve the financial freedom equation as rapidly as possible, with the greatest odds of success possible. But, this book speaks broadly to a national audience. It will be up to you to determine the path best suited to your circumstances, location, income level, and priorities.

The Components to the Financial Independence Equation

Component #1: Assets!

What is an asset?

In this book, an asset is something that produces income (or reduces expenses) or appreciates in value. An asset should ideally produce financial benefit for use in the near future to support one's lifestyle prior to retirement age. Investment or business income produced by these assets should require far less effort to maintain than the forty-plus hours per week that most full-time jobs demand. If it doesn't produce income, doesn't reduce your living expenses, or isn't increasing in value faster than inflation, it's not a real asset. In this book, we will distinguish between Real Assets (as defined above) and False Assets, as defined below.

Real assets for those interested in satisfying the financial independence equation include things like:

- Rental properties

- Stocks

- Bonds

- Publicly-traded securities

- Income-generating businesses

- Other assets that generate income and are expected to maintain or increase their value

False assets include things that are generally included on a balance sheet as a positive but which actually detract from the goal of achieving early financial freedom. Many other works in the world of finance include things under the bucket of "assets" that are not, in fact, real assets, at least not for the purposes of this book. Examples of these false assets include:

- Cars, boats, trucks, SUVs, RVs, or other luxury vehicles

- Homes

- College/graduate degrees

- Retirement accounts

- Computers

- Furniture

- Art and other collectables

These false assets require the owner to earn more cash or deplete their savings to purchase and maintain them, don't generate income, and in some cases lose value over time. For those pursuing early financial freedom, these purchases are liabilities, not assets. It can be difficult to stay away from these assets completely, but it must be totally clear to the purchaser their purchase will delay the attainment of financial freedom.

Now, to caveat this a little bit, understand that, yes, these items can be assets. A car or truck can be an asset, if it is used to drive other people around for a living. Art can be an asset, if the owner has a museum and charges others admission to come and see it. A home can be an asset if you rent out a room. The same goes for all the other assets listed here. But, be honest with yourself about the intent of your purchases. Are you buying a home, car, art, computer, or piece of furniture with the intention of deploying it as an income-producing asset? Or is it primarily for personal luxury and convenience? If you are not buying true assets, understand that false assets (liabilities) are a hindrance for those seeking early financial freedom.

Many people are unable to correctly distinguish between an asset and a liability in their personal lives. Americans in the middle class tend to accumulate liabilities at an alarming rate, all the while thinking, incorrectly, that these are smart "investments" that will "pay off in the long run."

There are three common false assets that many Americans are accumulating to disastrous financial consequence. These false assets are a financed car, a financed home, and a financed degree. Granted, some folks are content to sacrifice their balance sheets for the comforts and luxuries addressed below, and these purchases can make sense given personal goals outside of the pursuit of financial freedom. But, the items below shouldn't be considered assets and should be recognized for what they are: expensive luxuries that can delay financial freedom.

"False Asset" #1: A Financed Car

A financed car costs a tremendous amount of money per month, and in addition, incentivizes the use of vehicle transport more often because of the huge fixed expenses that come with vehicle ownership ("Well, I already paid for it. I might as well use it!"). On top of that, cars cost money per mile in the form of gas, maintenance, parking, and depreciation. All of this isn't to mention the subtler financial burdens of frequent driving, like increased insurance premiums and the increased risk of collision that increases with every mile driven.

Instead of buying a new car with a hefty loan, buy a reliable used economy car, like a five to ten-year-old Toyota Corolla, Honda Civic, Nissan Sentra, or other similarly low cost, highly reliable vehicle. Purchasing a first vehicle like this might have a far less negative impact on your finances than buying a brand new car with financing. Don't make the mistake of buying a new luxury vehicle believing that it will lead to lasting happiness or financial rewards.

"False Asset" #2: A Financed House

There are three ways to design your living situation: You can rent, you can buy a nice single family home or condo, or you can house hack. Renting is usually the worst long-term financial decision in most markets. Every dollar spent on rent is a 100 percent loss that's never seen again. From the standpoint of achieving financial freedom quickly, it is imperative to move away from the status of "tenant" as soon as practical.

It should already be quite clear that a primary residence occupied solely by one's family isn't an asset. It is a liability with negative cash flow. All else being equal, homeownership is usually superior to renting, but a huge amount of money in the form of mortgage payments, taxes, insurance, and monthly upkeep is spent each month. Furthermore, the equity built in a primary residence is rarely usable in the short term, without incurring more debt (in the form of a home equity loan or line of credit) that needs to be paid off when the home is sold.

Understand the difference between a real and a false asset, and seek the clearly superior alternative of turning your home into a real asset through house hacking (as described in chapter 4). Do this by intelligently buying small multifamily properties, or homes with extra rooms with the intention of renting them out. This can provide enough cash flow to pay down the mortgage and cover the mortgage payment and the operating costs of the property. If done correctly, the purchaser can cover the single largest expense in most American lives: housing.

"False Asset" #3: A Financed Advanced Degree

Education is great. There are myriad studies about how much more people make over the course of their careers when they go to college, graduate school, or secure specialty degrees such as becoming a doctor or lawyer. This isn't in dispute. It is absolutely true that over the course of a forty-year career, folks with an advanced degree can earn way more than their peers without such degrees.

But that's really only likely to be true over a long career. Remember, that's not going to be the case for those seeking to achieve early financial freedom. It's more likely that a "career" (the period during which one must rely on income from employment to sustain their lifestyle) will be under twenty, fifteen, or even ten years or less, for those attaining their goal of early financial freedom.

Those seeking financial freedom early in life are well served to be wary of expensive business schools, law schools, medical schools, or other advanced degrees. In most cases, time spent obtaining this schooling can significantly delay one's ability to accumulate wealth, as well as the corresponding passive income that can so greatly increase opportunity and free up time.

There are two main reasons why folks pursuing early financial freedom might want to watch out for financed education beyond a bachelor's degree at an economically priced institution:

- Reason #1: The Financial Costs. Graduate school is expensive; for example, the average debt load taken on by MBA graduates is $57,600,[2] though this will vary depending on the specific degree and university. On top of that, the student misses out on the potential income they could have earned and invested while studying and spending money on graduate school. If the goal is to become financially free as rapidly as possible, then graduate school is likely to slow, not speed, progress toward that goal. Of course, it's possible to graduate debt-free, for example by having an employer or family member pay for school. In that case, a free or low-cost degree that will result in a rapid increase in earnings may make sense. Just think through all the consequences before taking on tens of thousands of dollars in debt and committing many years of life to a specialized degree and ensuing specialized career.

- Reason #2: The Mental Costs of the Education. Suppose Stanford or Harvard accepts a high performer for business school. Two years later, this person might emerge with a degree from one of the finest institutions of business learning in the world, and ask

---

[2] Clark, *Debt Is Piling Up Faster for Most Graduate Students—but Not MBAs*, Online.

herself, "What's next?" Well, unfortunately, because she has a $200,000 degree from an elite school, every single option she had in life prior to getting that degree now makes less sense except for one: going to work at a high paying job with long hours at a large corporation. She has backed herself into a mental corner with that degree. She can't decide to work at a surf shop, take six months and backpack around Thailand, or even invest in low-end real estate. Those options, perfectly acceptable to millions around the world, are now no longer sensible for someone in her position! She's got an MBA from Harvard and can't accept a job that pays less than $100,000 per year. She certainly can't afford a job without prospects offering the opportunity to make far more than that a few years down the line. Instead, she will feel obligated to work a high paying job in a corporate, banking, or investment environment, using her high pay to begin eliminating her student loan debt.

Bonus "False Asset:": The Cash-flow Negative Spouse

You'll know this one when you see it. This is the husband who is too lazy to get a job and hits up the bar every night, or the stay-at-home mom who spends thousands on designer clothes and jewelry and expects a fancy dinner out at a nice restaurant every week.

It is imperative that both partners contribute to the family's bottom line either by contributing income or enforcing a budget and financial discipline. A lack of alignment can result in devastating consequences that not only leave couples in dire financial straits, it can potentially ruin the relationship.

This is probably the most important "asset" to avoid in gaining early financial freedom. If your spouse is as committed to helping the family achieve its long-term goals as you are, then avoiding the other "assets" on this list becomes much more achievable.

Wrapping Up False Assets

So, are you accumulating real assets or false ones as you go through life? Everyone makes mistakes. It's all about mitigating those mistakes, learning from them, and applying future capital to the things that will truly improve your life over the long run. Those are the real assets.

You don't need a car, a house on a hill, or a fancy degree. You can get around quickly, healthily, and for free on a bike, live for free in half of a duplex, and learn and network for free on the Internet and in your local community. Consider those things to be your assets.

Come on! My Parents/Grandparents/Everybody Else Can't All Be Wrong!

The two false assets that tend to be the most confusing to folks who are trying to achieve early financial freedom are also the areas where the middle-class American tends to accumulate all or most of its wealth. These two things are:

- Home equity

- Retirement accounts

I can almost hear a chorus of you saying, "But wait! What about all the great things I've read from so many other folks about why I should save for retirement and about how important retirement accounts are?" And too, "What about all the people out there who swear their home is the best investment they've ever made?"

As a caveat to this section, it isn't *bad* to have home equity or retirement savings. They just aren't particularly useful assets in the short-medium term. If the plan is to create a life of financial freedom twenty, thirty, or even forty years before the age of retirement, then home equity and retirement savings aren't really going to help. Therefore, making choices that result in building wealth primarily in two places where said wealth is relatively inaccessible is a pretty lousy strategy. Think about it: If money is in a retirement account, there is an implicit assumption a reasonable person can make that this money isn't likely to be used until retirement age.

There are only a few ways to harness home equity in the pursuit of financial freedom: One, you can sell the property, take the cash out, and invest it somewhere else. Let's be real, however, the vast majority of folks with significant home equity built that equity by living in their home and paying down their mortgages. Likely, they plan to continue living in their home for a long time. Few pursue early financial freedom with a plan to buy a big, fancy home in a nice area, pay down the mortgage every month, pray the home increases in value, sell it off, and then downgrade by renting a cheap apartment or smaller home. This would be a fairly absurd plan, as it's possible to move toward early financial freedom far faster by buying the smaller home to begin with and investing aggressively in assets like stocks. Homes are historically unlikely to produce wealth at a faster rate than other types of easily accessible investments. Instead, many folks tend to buy a nice place, live there for a few years, and then use that home equity as part of the purchase of another home, usually a larger one, sometime in the future. For these folks, their home equity will not positively contribute to early financial freedom.

The second way to harness home equity is to borrow against it. Borrowing against home equity to fund luxuries like a new car or boat is directly counter to the goal of early financial freedom, and therefore isn't going to be discussed further in this book. However, those who already have a lot of equity in their primary residence may be able to borrow against it at low rates to invest in other ventures. For example, they might be able to borrow against their home equity to invest in a rental property that would yield positive cash flow immediately.

Finally, home equity can aid in early financial freedom if the home is paid off in full. If the mortgage is paid off entirely, then the mortgage payment (a major drain on cash flow) is eliminated. Understand, however, that the owner of a home worth $400,000, that's fully paid off, *forgoes earning investment income* on that $400,000. It might well be possible to invest that $400,000 and earn $30,000, $40,000, or more per year if it's invested in index funds producing between 7.5 percent and 10 percent annual returns. Homes on the other hand, typically tend to appreciate at around 3 to 5 percent, at best, over time ($12,000 to $20,000 per year in this example), which is less than half of the returns historically produced by the stock market. While it's likely more efficient to develop other streams of income before paying off the mortgage entirely, it's popular among folks who are already financially independent or close to eliminate personal debts, including their home mortgage.

Chapter 5 discusses real estate decisions in depth, so the important takeaway here is simply that owning your own home outright isn't a no-brainer. It just happens to be considered a "great investment" by many people because they have never made an investment of similar scale. Folks who have only made one large investment (their home purchase) are likely to argue the home is a great investment because they have little experience with other investments.

Similarly, retirement savings that that won't be accessed for several decades (assuming "retirement" from wage-paying work at a young age) aren't much use. Build wealth, which generates accessible returns in a more deliberate, intelligent manner. This should be wealth that can be spent today, penalty-free. The Appendix discusses in more detail how to intelligently take advantage of the rules surrounding retirement accounts so they *can* be accessed for early financial freedom.

Middle-class America has built most of its wealth in retirement accounts and home equity simply because the decision to contribute is automatic and long term. Every paycheck, millions of Americans contribute a small amount to a 401(k) or retirement account. Every month, millions of Americans pay a small amount toward a large mortgage. This happens like clockwork. Do not manage wealth this way. Instead, intentionally build wealth in a readily accessible form, and accumulate assets that are likely to produce excellent results that provide benefits immediately.

How to Acquire Assets

Thinking in terms of acquiring real assets requires a fundamental shift in perspective. Stop thinking that the financial goal is to max out retirement contributions, make a mortgage payment, and put away a small amount for savings each month. Stop hoping that compound interest will result in wealth in the long run.

Instead, put away a huge chunk toward savings and easily-accessible, investable wealth every month by completing parts I and II of this book, and then, if there is money left over, pay for things like retirement contributions.

There are many ways to accumulate assets that don't involve accumulating cash first. But, the best way for the W2 employee to rapidly move toward financial freedom is to simply spend less than they earn, or earn more than they spend,

In case you were wondering, here are some other ways in which one might acquire assets:

- Investing or reinvesting returns from other assets

- Building a business or passive income stream from scratch

- Receiving assets as a gift/inheritance

- Being compensated (paid) for work performed with equity or ownership in assets, in addition to or instead of a paycheck

While these are all possible, these methods of accumulating assets are often immaterial (if you have no or few assets, then you won't have any significant returns to reinvest . . .), are outside the control of a typical W2 employee's life (you are either getting an inheritance or you aren't, and, in most cases, can't predict the timing of these things), or are not practical given the demands and constraints of a typical full-time job. The two areas that are within the individual's control, however, are how much one earns (*you always control this in the long run*) and usually to an even greater extent, how much one spends (*you always control this*).

Put yourself in a position where you are routinely capable of purchasing intelligent, sensible assets that make sense in getting you where you want to go.

Component #2: Returns

From the standpoint of achieving financial freedom at an early age, the point of accumulating assets is to generate cash flow to supplement or replace wage income, and to generate long-term wealth in the form of appreciation. Do not save money for the sake of saving money. Save money to invest it, and generate cash flow and appreciation.

Investment returns are critical to wealth generation, *but only for those who have significant assets with which to invest.* Some people will be looking to this book hoping to score some great investment tips. This book has nothing to offer those looking to make a quick buck in the stock market. Attempting to earn outsized investment returns in a traditional sense is actually the least relevant goal for the typical reader of this book (with net worth of less than $100,000) in the initial years of wealth building.

Yes, earning excellent investment returns is an important component of any successful wealth-building plan, and, yes, chapter 9 will go into great detail about investing. But, the key thing is that *even excellent investment returns don't matter if the amount of money invested is too small.*

If Bryan has a stockpile of $1000, and doubles that money in the stock market, his life won't change much. Sure, he has an extra thousand dollars, but he cannot quit his job, cannot move and sustain significantly higher rent or mortgage payments, and cannot change material aspects of his transportation or other daily activities over the long run. Same thing with $10,000.

But, if Bryan can take $100,000 and invest it efficiently, earning steady 10 to 15 percent returns, all of a sudden he may experience a real impact on his life. He's now earning about $1000 *per month*, an amount of money that could very well positively influence major life decisions. Investing is extremely important, but to have a real impact at getting him to a life changing amount of wealth, he must aggressively stockpile cash by earning and saving first—and fast. Yes, you can and should invest every dollar above and beyond what you need to get by, even if you are starting from scratch, but the return on your savings shouldn't be a heavy focus until you have a substantial amount saved.

Investment returns are usually expressed in terms of percentages. If someone says they earn 10 percent annual returns, it means that for every $100 invested, they both keep their initial $100 and they build an additional $10 in wealth, annually. Be careful anytime percentages are used to demonstrate return. Investment opportunities should be prioritized, not just by the percentage return offered, but by the materiality of those returns as well. For example, it's clearly preferable to invest $10,000 and earn a return of $2000, than to invest $10 and return $20, assuming both investments produced those returns over the course of a full year. It's obviously silly to brag about a 200-percent return on a $10 investment, and clearly more worthwhile to achieve a 20 percent return on a $10,000 investment.

Similarly ridiculous, but far more common, is the case where a young investor will strive to increase investment returns on a fledgling portfolio of stocks worth $10,000 or less by a few percentage points. For every 1 percent increase in returns the investor boasts about a $100-per-year increase in wealth. That same increase in wealth could be generated by a single night of tending bar, driving for Uber, or a single day of working an event where labor is needed.

It is far more efficient to build wealth by seeking other ways to earn additional cash, until your portfolio reaches significant scale. Think of earning investment returns as you would go about accepting wages. Don't put in the work to achieve an extra 1 percent return on $1000 invested ($10) when you could simply go earn money far more efficiently.

On the other hand, portfolios with a certain scale (often $100,000 or more) can often produce annual returns of $10,000, $20,000, or much more by creative and successful investors. All of a sudden, this becomes an effort that's actually rewarding. Regardless of current portfolio size, it's always valuable to self-educate on the fundamentals of investing and wealth management. One of the best ways to do this is to aggressively save and earn, and to use small amounts of money to try new strategies and hone your investing skills in ways that you expect will provide future benefit.

Those just starting out with little to invest, however, would be well served to focus the bulk of their efforts on earning more money instead of attempting to eke out large percentage returns on fledgling portfolios.

The Safe Withdrawal Rate

The safe withdrawal rate (SWR), expressed as a percentage, determines what percent of usable net worth ("real" assets) that can be withdrawn each year, such that your assets are not depleted. The SWR is defined as the quantity of money, expressed as a percentage of the initial investment, which can be withdrawn per year for a given quantity of time, including adjustments for inflation, and not lead to portfolio failure. You can use the safe withdrawal rate to answer the question: "How much wealth do I need to accumulate to become financially free with little to no risk?" It corresponds to the "returns" variable in the financial freedom equation. The safe withdrawal rate is a number *you* choose. It is a rate of return that the individual investor accepts, such that she might have excellent odds of never depleting her asset base.

A conservative person might assume a safe withdrawal rate of 1 to 2 percent. This means that if this person wants an annual income of $50,000, he should accumulate $2.5M to $5M in assets. Another way to put this is that someone assuming a safe withdrawal rate of 1 percent will need to build up 100 times their spending in real assets prior to leaving wage-paying work.

An aggressive person with a $50,000 per year lifestyle might assume a 10 percent safe withdrawal rate. This person might quit his job at $500,000 in assets. This person needs to build up ten times their spending prior to leaving wage paying work.

The overly-cautious investor delays financial freedom needlessly, while the overly-aggressive investor risks having to return to wage-paying work or cut back on the desired lifestyle if those high returns are unable to be sustained. However, this isn't a pass/fail test. Wealth, spending, and the safe withdrawal rate are a continuum. Withdrawing slightly too much money doesn't have devastating financial consequences, just as a slightly too conservative safe withdrawal rate will likely not result in decades of needless additional work.

For example, if Melinda leaves her wage-paying job between thirty and forty years of age at $1M in assets and a $50,000-per-year lifestyle, she has multiple options if the market crashes and her assets are no longer able to support her lifestyle. The first option is to simply cut back on her lifestyle. Instead of living on $50,000 per year, she might simply live on $40,000 per year. This would work well if her portfolio fell to $800,000 in value and she continued operating with a 5 percent safe withdrawal rate. The second option is to simply return to part-time or even full-time wage-paying work for a short period until she regained confidence in her financial position or her assets recover in value.

Those who plan to start a business or work freelance might be comfortable transitioning out of their wage-paying jobs with far fewer assets built up. Those willing to take on some part-time work in years where investments yield poor returns, or those willing to spend less and live even more frugally during those periods, can assume a higher safe withdrawal rate and achieve financial freedom earlier than someone who is more conservative.

Many experts will suggest different numbers. Some suggest that investors expect no greater than 2 percent annual returns, while others suggest that average investors can expect greater than 7 percent annual returns. Those who are young and confident in their ability to return to high paying work or intend to immediately start a business might be comfortable exiting the workforce at a 10 percent safe withdrawal rate. Those aspiring to early financial freedom with more flexibility may want to consider assuming a 5 percent safe withdrawal rate as a reasonable middle ground. Having completed parts I and II of this book, your lifestyle should cost somewhere between $2000 and $3000 or less per month, or $25,000 to $36,000 per year. Assuming a 5 percent safe withdrawal rate, you will need to accumulate $500,000 to $720,000 in wealth to confidently leave wage-paying work.

Component #3: Lifestyle

The third parameter of the financial independence equation is the annual cost of the lifestyle that's desired. Obviously, the return on assets needed to satisfy a low-cost lifestyle are less than those needed to satisfy a high-cost one. The reason frugality was discussed in the very first chapter of this book is because the cost of one's lifestyle will be the single largest determinant of when they achieve early financial freedom.

Remember, at a safe withdrawal rate of 5 percent, each additional dollar spent on lifestyle expenses increases the amount of assets needed to achieve financial freedom *twentyfold*. Every $100 per month in additional expense means $1200 per year in expense, or *$24,000* in real wealth needed to sustain early financial freedom. That's a lot of money. It's the first *year* of savings we described in part I. The more streamlined your personal spending and lifestyle, the less you spend keeping afloat month to month, the easier it will be to achieve early financial freedom. Think carefully about each part of your budget, and constantly prune unnecessary expenses. Your *spending* is likely to be the single greatest barrier between you and early financial freedom.

And remember, once you achieve early financial freedom, you can always continue to work and pile on assets. Just make sure that your spending increases only in proportion to your wealth. If you retire, and *then* build a business or realize incredible growth from your assets, you can always increase spending with the excess cash flow. The guy with $10M in wealth and even average investment returns can conservatively fund a $200,000 per year lifestyle and continue to grow increasingly wealthy, even relative to inflation.

Lifestyle is covered in great detail in part I, and you are invited to refer back to that section at your leisure.

Conclusion

Are you acquiring real assets or false assets in your life? Are the assets on your personal balance sheet working for you, or are you forced to spend your current cash flow to maintain them? To achieve early financial freedom, you will need to transform your financial position from one with little to no real assets or one dominated by false assets to one in which you have a large amount of real wealth that generates income and appreciates in value forever.

This all starts with lifestyle. Those living a low-cost lifestyle need fewer real assets and can earn lower returns on those assets to sustain early financial freedom. A low-cost lifestyle enables the saver to accumulate cash and income producing assets faster. And, a low-cost lifestyle with a large cash cushion has a long runway before running into financial problems. These advantages are enormous.

However, once assets begin to accumulate, and as options and opportunity present themselves, it's not enough to save one's way to early financial freedom. The focus needs to shift away from an automated low-cost lifestyle to the purchase and creation of real assets that generate income. There are a wide variety of ways that the seeker of early financial freedom can solve the financial freedom equation, but they must keep in mind the fact that only assets that generate income or appreciate in value faster than inflation count toward their early financial freedom.

Chapter 9
An Introduction to Investing for Early Financial Freedom

For the purpose of this book, the goal of investing is to continually build real assets with returns sufficient to sustain early financial freedom. The goal here is not to help you "get rich" on a homerun shot, or to "preserve capital" (until you acquire a meaningful amount of wealth, that is). While those are viable goals for some, they may not be appropriate for folks seeking early financial freedom. They also may not be sustainable goals. The point of this entire book is to rapidly attain a state of early financial freedom from a standing start of little to no assets. It's not acceptable to generate a large amount of wealth in a short period of time, but then not realize consistent returns on that wealth once one has left wage-paying work for good. An acceptably fast and high probability way to achieve your goal is to aggressively and consistently invest, reinvest, and rapidly accelerate according to a winning formula.

Those looking to begin investing will, at the very least, want to boast a financial position in which they have plenty of cash on hand, with a large monthly surplus. Do not begin making large investments if you have outstanding bad debts remaining. Do not begin making large investments if you don't have thousands or preferably tens of thousands of dollars in accessible wealth—if a problem or life opportunity comes up that requires use of the invested funds, you may be forced to sell off the investment early and at a loss to access your cash. Do not begin making large investments that might produce negative cash flows (forcing you to plow more money into them) if you are not consistently cash flow positive in your personal life.

If you have built up the cash reserve described in part I and are continuing at your wage-paying job, you are likely in a strong personal financial position to aggressively begin investing. It is time to focus your attention on learning how to invest in a systematic manner that will give you the best chance of efficiently building wealth.

Note that those who have completed parts I and II of this book may also find themselves in excellent position to take on entrepreneurial pursuits, including starting and buying small businesses. While this book isn't aimed at entrepreneurs, the more one's personal financial position advances, the more they decrease their personal financial risk when starting a business. You are enabled to pursue entrepreneurship in part due to your continually lengthening financial runway. The guy with over $100,000 in real net worth has a four-year financial runway on a $25,000 per year lifestyle. That means he can work on a new business for years before running out of capital and needing to return to wage-paying work. Compare that to the fellow with no real net worth, who is forced to raise money or work around his day job. The lines between creative investing and entrepreneurship can be blurry. Understand that as someone who is ready to begin making material investments, you are also in a strong position to buy or build small businesses, if you choose to put in the extra effort needed to manage them.

Traditional retirement planning and investing makes little sense for those aspiring to early financial freedom and produces financial freedom at a much slower rate. Understand that the investment strategy described in this book will differ dramatically from the advice given by Average Joe's financial planner. Average Joe gets average advice. Remember that Average Joe also doesn't have $100,000 in net worth that directly works toward his early retirement.

For those seeking early and permanent financial freedom, there are some tenets that will aid in making excellent decisions. These are the seven core tenets of investing. Violate these tenets, and you risk slowing your journey to early financial freedom. After that, we will explore key investing concepts that will help you frame your investment ideology. But first, we need to understand the implications of inflation. Let's do that next.

Inflation

The inflation rate is the rise in the price of goods and services over time, as evidenced by the fact that it costs more to buy things like a house, car, milk, food today than it did 100 years ago. While inflation increases are irregular, prices across a basket of goods and services have actually been measured for decades to help us gain a better understanding of inflation.

This index, called the Consumer Price Index, suggests that the inflation rate averages out to about 3.2 percent per year over the past several decades. This means that prices will double about every twenty years or so.

Because of inflation, the value of cash decreases over time, as it will purchase fewer and fewer goods and services. Therefore, holding wealth in cash in an inflammatory period results in a situation where we are almost certain to become poorer over time.

Investing should produce income or appreciation in excess of inflation, such that our assets can fund our ever-inflating lifestyle expenses forever. At minimum, investments need to keep pace with inflation.

The Seven Core Tenets of Investing

To kick things off, here's the list:

- Tenet #1: *Never* spend the principal
- Tenet #2: *Reinvest* most investment returns
- Tenet #3: To invest, one must have capital
- Tenet #4: Effort correlates with return only if you are in control of the investment
- Tenet #5: Investment returns are impacted by knowledge
- Tenet #6: Do not confuse volatility with risk
- Tenet #7: The best investments are specific to the investor's personal situation

Tenet #1: Never Spend the Principal

In part I, we built up $25,000 in readily accessible wealth. That reserve is for your use when life's opportunities or challenges come your way. That cash is to be used toward the purchase of a primary residence or house hack. That cash is to be used for a financial runway. It isn't to be tied up in an investment. That cash is for *spending*, where that spending will give you a significant financial advantage. When you begin investing—actually buying assets that you hope to sustain your lifestyle for the rest of your life, you *never, ever* plan on spending the invested dollars.

Successful investors understand this fundamental concept to the core. In fact, it's the root of capitalism, and the great divide between the 1 percent and everyone else. To sum up the key to wealth *preservation* in one phrase:

Never, ever spend the principal. Abide by this rule and you, your children, and your children's children will be taken care of financially until the end of time.

When you decide to invest a dollar, you need to think of that dollar as gone. Out of your life. Forever. You never get to spend that dollar. You never use it to buy coffee, purchase a primary residence, pay for Junior's college, spend on retirement expenses, or anything else. Instead that dollar is to be put to work generating returns, forever.

It is acceptable to spend the returns generated by an investment though, whenever they materialize. But it's not acceptable to spend the original dollar if your goal is to sustain a perpetual state of financial freedom. Invested dollars or assets must be continually allowed to generate returns forever. Let's explore this concept with an example.

> *Kristi saved up $100,000 and buys a rental property for the same amount. A year goes by and the property has generated $500 per month in cash flow, and the property is now worth $103,000, as it has appreciated in value. She sells the property, collects her cash, and walks away.*
>
> *Her situation a year from now is this: she has $106,000 in the bank. After accounting for taxes (let's say in this example that her she owes 33 percent of her gain in taxes) her return includes the $6,000 in rental income and the $3,000 in appreciation—a total pre-tax gain of $9,000, which equates to a 6 percent return on investment (ROI) after taxes. The other $100,000 of that money in the bank is the principal she used to invest in the first place.*

Here are the results:

- *$106,000 in the bank*
- *$100,000 was the principal, or initial amount invested*
- *$6,000 is rental income ($500 per month for twelve months)*
- *$3,000 is appreciation capital gains*
- *$6,000 investment return, net after the 33 percent tax she pays.*

Kristi can spend the $6,000 that she generated from this property without depleting her wealth, but if she spends more than that, then she has less than she started with. Kristi is an investor and wouldn't even for a second consider spending anything beyond that $6,000. The original $100,000 isn't to be touched and instead should be reinvested in the next property or other income-generating asset. To spend that money would violate the first core tenet of investing—and instead of building wealth, she'd destroy it.

Investors who are successful over the long term don't get into that situation. They have their personal finances arranged to the point where they won't be forced to liquidate their investments to pay for life's curveballs.

Tenet #2: Reinvest Most Investment Returns

If you want to build wealth, you can't just spend all of the returns generated by your investments. Instead, you need to reinvest at least a portion of the return. Back to the example of the rental property above. If Kristi increases her wealth from $100,000 to $106,000 as a result of her investment, she can't expect to get any richer by spending that $6,000! Instead, she needs to reinvest part of that $6,000 and for say, a $104,000 property. The larger, nicer house will generate more rent and perhaps more dollar gains in appreciation than the first one, and her wealth will grow faster and faster as she repeats this.

While it's impossible to achieve financial freedom without, at some point, living off investment returns, the key is to get to a point where a majority of the investment returns are reinvested. This can be achieved by assuming a reasonably conservative safe withdrawal rate, discussed in the previous chapter. The key is that you can spend the safe withdrawal rate when you achieve financial freedom—that's the whole point!

In the case of the house in the example above, Kristi could still build sufficient wealth by spending just $2,000 of that $6,000 return, and reinvesting the balance. When she is financially free, she'll just need to make sure she never spends more than the total return generated by her investments such that she dips into the principal.

The point of investing is to achieve early financial freedom, so make sure to enjoy the benefits. Be careful not to spend the principal, and on your way to early financial freedom make sure to reinvest the majority of the returns.

Tenet #3: To Invest, One Must Have Capital

You cannot invest money unless you have money to invest with. And you cannot accumulate capital without earning it (or inheriting it) and keeping it. You have to start somewhere. This is why there is such a great divide of wealth in America. In spite of incredible advantages, most Americans fail to accumulate significant capital early in their lives. However, by following the process in parts I and II of this book, you will be able to break the mold and accumulate a large amount of capital over a short period of time.

Want to get into investing, building wealth, and achieving financial freedom? Then *keep* the money you earn. Don't spend it. Master the other sections of this book first, build up your reserves, and then seek to become an avid investor. Don't fool yourself into believing you are investing when others contribute the capital for an investment. Don't be fooled by others who call themselves investors, yet, don't have any personal wealth. Understand that an investor invests his or her *own* capital. While this tenet may seem obvious, the title of "investor" is often bestowed upon folks who merely manage other people's money. These people don't invest, they manage.

An investor doesn't accept someone else's money and invest it in an enterprise, just as an employee isn't an investor when he or she accepts stock options at a company. When this happens, the individual is beholden to another individual or company and responsible to them for results. When one is responsible for delivering financial results to outside investors, they are in direct violation of the goal of early financial freedom. An investor invests cash or equivalents, and accumulates that cash either from prior investments or other sources, such as wage-paying work or business income.

When seeking investment advice, understand whether or not it's coming from an individual who's an investor or an imposter. And, more importantly, don't fool yourself into thinking that you're investing when you manage other people's money. Early financial freedom is achieved when you accumulate your own assets, and then invest and reinvest.

Tenet #4: Effort Correlates with Return Only If You Are in Control of the Investment

Ever met someone who spends a lot of time talking about stock picks and his fledgling portfolio? Someone who meticulously studies the market, looking for undervalued stocks? That guy probably puts in a lot of effort. And enthusiasm. And brainpower. And he's probably got this righteous attitude about how he's doing it better than everyone else. Unfortunately for him, he's wasting his time.

His efforts picking stocks, one at a time, timing markets, and otherwise trying to outperform Wall Street funds are utterly wasted, as he could have otherwise simply invested in a market index fund and likely earned superior long-term returns. (This will be explained in more detail later.) It is interesting to write about this topic because many low net worth investors get riled up when they hear that something they put a lot of time and effort into is statistically worthless.

Keep in mind that any investment that outpaces inflation can make you wealthy. Even lousy investors can become wealthy, so long as they reinvest most of their returns and at least beat inflation over the long run. Unfortunately, the fact that successful stock pickers can become wealthy tricks many investors into believing that security analysis (trying to find undervalued stocks with the hopes that they go up in value more than other stocks in the marketplace), or stock trading is a productive pursuit.

Luckily, you won't be one of those folks because you recognize that—unless you want to devote a career to Wall Street and learn to live and breathe the nuances of public markets, or alternatively, spend a lifetime finding, managing, and systematically buying and improving excellent companies—you'd be better off investing in index funds.

Far too many amateur investors attempt to pick stocks and beat the experts in public markets. And there is simply no correlation between their efforts and outsized returns. The problem here is that when folks invest in publicly traded stocks and bonds, other people control the fate of their investment. Other people are responsible for the results of the company, the repayment of debt, and the success of a given financial instrument.

Now, effort can improve the results of your investment, if you have control over the investment. For example, if you own a piece of real estate and fix it up yourself, you may find yourself earning $50, $100, or $250 an hour through your labor. If you earn less than that at your day job, then your efforts are indeed providing outsized returns for you.

Tenet #5: Investment Returns Are Impacted by Knowledge

Interestingly, one of the reasons folks attempt to pick stocks is because they haven't bothered to read dozens of books on investing. They are ignorant of the math and philosophy behind why successful investors suggest not doing things like picking stocks. Thus, it's their lack of knowledge that leads to subpar investment results.

Investors know that knowledge can be incredibly powerful to their long-term financial positions and investment returns—if applied correctly to businesses they have some control over. For example, a knowledgeable real estate investor with a strong understanding of real estate investing fundamentals and the local market has an excellent chance to produce consistently strong returns. This investor might be able to efficiently manage the rehab of dilapidated properties, or operate an effective landlording business. On the other hand, a stock picker can merely hope that management of a company and public sentiment drives the prices of his security up.

While a real estate investor might put in some effort in the form of labor and management of the property, most of her effort involves becoming deeply familiar with the fundamentals of real estate investing. Everything from how to market and how to analyze a property to how to screen tenants, protect the property, do due diligence, as well as read and study contracts.

That type of effort involves accumulating knowledge. The physical exertions and time spent actually working on the investment—individual efforts—can be almost entirely outsourced to property managers, handymen, and contractors, and as investors grow wealthy, this effort should be hired out. However, without knowledge so much can go wrong for those who seek to invest and build businesses. Knowledge decreases the risk of an investment in which an investor has control. Failing to accumulate knowledge can reduce returns, and can even cause an investor to lose the invested principal.

Tenet #6: Investors Do Not Confuse Volatility with Risk

"Aren't stocks risky?" A common conviction among many investors is that stocks are, generally speaking, riskier investments than bonds. Whether or not an investment is risky depends on what is meant by risk. Stocks, in comparison to bonds, are *not risky*. Folks who say this don't understand the definition of risk very well, or are using a definition of risk that doesn't apply to someone with the goal of early and lasting financial freedom.

Now, stocks as a group are more volatile than bonds. However, it's important to make the distinction between *risk* and *volatility*, a distinction many investors fail to adequately understand.

While stocks are more volatile than bonds, they are not more risky. Financial advisors, major media outlets, and consequently, many investors, have it drilled into their heads that stocks are riskier than bonds. This leads them to make decisions that significantly cost them in both the short and long term.

Let's use a graph to demonstrate this point:

Value of $100 - Stocks Vs T-Bonds

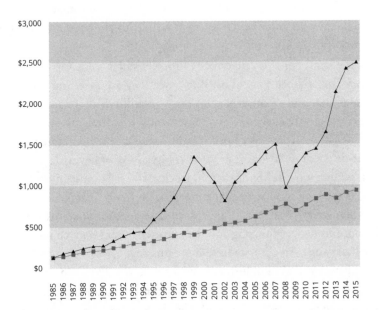

The chart shows the total compounded value of an investment in treasury bonds versus an equivalent starting investment in stocks. The data is available at NYU's Stern School of Business.[1] The most noticeable feature of this graph is that treasury bonds produced far less total return than stocks over the time period studied. This same scenario plays out across virtually every thirty-year period in modern history.

But an adherent to the "stocks are riskier than bonds" school of thought would counter that observation by pointing out the second most noticeable characteristic of the graph— Treasury bills also didn't suffer any huge losses (the dips in the stocks line) in the graph above. And they're right! But here's the thing: Investors, attempting to *permanently build sustainable sources of life changing passive income,* understand the core concept of investing. The first and most important core tenet: *Never, ever spend the principal.*

---

[1] Damodaran, *Damodaran Online,* Online.

Forever, (think, "never, ever") is a long time. Investors who are success-ful over the long term live off a portion of the cash flows and/or returns from their investments. Therefore, they only care about how investments will perform over the very long-term. Thus, investors only care about the first observation in the graph. They care only that an investment helps them build the most total wealth over time, relative to its alternatives. Stocks, over every long period of time, have historically produced more wealth than bonds, and with increasing statistical certainty the longer the time horizon! It is therefore quite costly to allow the secondary point—that stock values will fluctuate with more volatility than bonds, to supersede the most im-portant point!

In the short run, yes, investors will likely suffer some big drops in the market value of stock portfolios. But, since they are investing forever, and never spend the principal, they accept that volatility with the understanding that they are clearly likely to build more wealth over time investing in stocks versus bonds! Another way of putting this is to say that bonds are *more* risky than stocks, because investors are at a far higher risk of having less long-term wealth by investing in bonds than in stocks. This is because investors in the game for the long term sensibly define "risk" as *"the probability of having less wealth over time."* With this more appropriate definition, bonds are statisti-cally more risky over the long run than stocks. Stocks may be more *volatile* in the short-run—stocks may have more ups and downs—but over virtually every thirty-year period in history, equity markets outperform debt markets!

Understand your time horizon. A young investor may plan to live to be a hundred years old, and therefore might have an investing time horizon of seventy to seventy-five years. A fifty-year-old investor might plan for a time horizon of at least fifty years. Too many so-called "investors" plan to retire at sixty-five and hope that their money doesn't run out before they die. How dangerous to plan to live to eighty—it's well possible that one dies much younger or lives much longer. It can only make sense then, to live a wonderful life in the present, but plan financially to live and invest forever.

Note: If you plan to *spend* the principal of an investment, then the defi-nition of risk introduced here doesn't apply to you. Remember, according to Tenet #1, you aren't investing if you plan to spend the principal. Instead, you are "saving" and you are in violation of that core tenet of investing.

Understand risk. Risk must be considered in relation to your time horizon. Over a long time horizon (the rest of your life, for example) vola-tility in the short run is tolerable. A voluntary, statistically certain long-term underperformance in return is not.

Tenet #7: The Best Investments Are Specific to the Investor's Personal Situation

Most people, especially amateur investors, fail to understand that great investment returns do not come from typical investments made in the stock market, bond markets, or even in real estate. Instead, the greatest investments are often in things that reduce monthly personal expenses. Yes, reducing monthly cash outflows counts as an increase in wealth and can be considered to be an investment return. If it allows for faster wealth accumulation than any other investment, then do it—and do it first!

> *Walker saved up $250. While he had the option to invest in the stock market, he instead opted to purchase a nice used bicycle on Craigslist. His commute is five miles, and his cost of commuting by car is about $.50 per mile. Biking to work thus saves him $5 per day or about $750 per year, assuming that he bikes 75 percent of the 200 workdays per year. That's an annual return of 300 percent, not counting the added benefits to his health. Walker is a serious student of financial freedom, and this was a serious investment he analyzed prior to working on income-producing investments.*

Similarly, one could spend some time and money filling their home with LED light bulbs, which burn far less energy than incandescent bulbs. They might invest in some cookware that will encourage them to prepare meals instead of eating out. And, instead of buying a true rental property "investment," they could buy a house and rent out the extra bedrooms, or even better, buy a multiplex, and rent out the extra space.

These *are* investments! Too few people give investments that save money the respect they deserve. They become very excited about owning popular companies like Facebook or Amazon, but refuse to believe purchases that substantially reduce their monthly expenses are investments. In many cases, they can earn far greater returns (ROI of 1000 percent or more) than stocks, bonds, and real estate. In a sense, part I of this book *is* an introduction to investing, as is the chapter on house hacking. Smart purchases can drastically reduce expenses (think of the benefits explained earlier of living closer to your work place), decreasing the amount of passive income needed to fund a lifestyle, and increasing one's ability to accumulate cash to invest in other assets.

It's foolish to even think about investing in any traditional sense if there is perfectly good money that's being thrown away each month. Often, this money can be saved with far less sacrifice than the time spent working hard to earn it or the time spent acquiring the knowledge needed to be a successful investor.

Reducing expenses is also advantageous with respect to taxes. For a median earner, income might be taxed at around a 30 percent marginal rate. In this scenario, the earner only keeps $.70 for each additional dollar in income. This earner would be far better off saving a dollar than earning an additional one, as he'd get to keep the whole thing! It's far more advantageous to save money than to earn it for most wage earners, dollar for dollar. When prioritizing investments, one that saves money should be prioritized over one that produces the same amount in income.

Five Concepts for the Savvy Investor

If you follow the core tenets, you will be off to a good start in developing a strategic investment plan, and will be able to think for yourself throughout your life about how to make intelligent use of your money. However, there are several additional points to consider as an investor. To that end, we are going to talk about five additional concepts that you need to understand when making investment decisions. These five concepts are:

- Speculation versus Investment
- Opportunity Cost
- Diversification
- Passive Income
- Materiality vs. ROI

Speculation versus Investment

Has anyone ever told you to consider investing in gold?

Gold is a rock (okay, it's technically a metal, but come on). It sits there. It shines. It produces no value, saves no lives, and does *nothing* but look good. Even that part about "looking good" is debatable. Here's Warren Buffet (widely considered to be the world's leading expert on the subject of investing for the long-term, and one of the wealthiest people in the world) on gold:

> *I will say this about gold. If you took all the gold in the world, it would roughly make a cube sixty-seven feet on a side. [. . .] Now for that same cube of gold, it would be worth at today's market*

prices about $7 trillion—that's probably about a third of the value of all the stocks in the United States. [. . .] For $7 trillion . . . you could have all the farmland in the United States, you could have about seven Exxon Mobils, and you could have a trillion dollars of walking-around money. [. . .] And if you offered me the choice of looking at some 67-foot cube of gold and looking at it all day, and you know me, touching it and fondling it occasionally . . . Call me crazy, but I'll take the farmland and the Exxon Mobils.[2]

Gold isn't an investment. When you hoard gold, you produce no value. At best, you are gambling that its price will go up relative to the currency you traded for it. This is called speculation. People can make money speculating, and it can be wise to speculate to a certain degree on things like real estate (buying a home in part of town that based on your research you think is likely to improve in the coming years, for example). But, while one may become a great businesswoman, a student of the market, and perhaps even become quite wealthy as a speculator, a speculator isn't an investor.

Speculation isn't a recipe, a formula, for long-term wealth and financial success that will compound forever and last for generations. Eventually, speculators lose their edge on the market; sustained, long-term success is only achieved with consistently applied effort, in much the same way that success in sales or a career relies on long term effort.

While it's wise to invest for the long term and to avoid speculation in forming a *strategy*, do not take that logic to an extreme where easy short-term wins are overlooked. Excellent and creative investors tend to be deal-finders and go-getters. It may be wise to purchase a short-term asset opportunistically (perhaps you find a great deal on a house, car, collectible) and resell it for a quick gain. Take advantage of easy wins in carefully researched areas of expertise, as they present themselves. But, an investment strategy should not *depend*, long-term, on finding incredible value and immediately realizing gain.

Your *strategy* should instead revolve around mathematical principles, which, applied over time, can lead to incredible long-term wealth in a sustainable and repeatable manner. It should revolve around the acquisition of assets that cannot only provide passive income to fund your current lifestyle, but allow for a likelihood of perpetual growth in both value and cash flow.

Pounce on a great deal if you spot one. But do not depend on finding great deals to make your strategy work. If an average investor can't win with

---

[2] Merriman, *The genius of Warren Buffett in 23 quotes,* Online.

your strategy over the long term, you need to find a new way to invest, assuming you desire largely passive income.

Opportunity Cost

Opportunity cost refers to a benefit that a person could have received, but gave up to take another course of action. Opportunity cost can be defined simply as the cost of *not* doing something. It is the cost of inaction. Or more precisely, the cost of failing to perform the optimal action. There are three types of opportunity cost to consider:

- Leaving money on the table
- Failing to invest
- Investing sub-optimally and the cost of capital

Leaving Money on the Table

A few years ago, Brock bought a duplex that needed some repairs in one unit. Brock lived in half of the duplex and rented out the extra bedroom in the unit to a friend for $550 per month. He decided to fix the property up himself, went to Home Depot, picked up some tools, and got to work. After making about 90 percent of the repairs, he got stuck on one of the repairs, lost interest, and pursued other activities, letting half of the property sit vacant for four months. Brock didn't think it was a big deal the property was vacant and figured he'd get around to it sooner or later.

One day, Brock came to a sharp realization. He realized *"Whoa, I'm literally throwing away $1000 per month, every month I don't find tenants to live in that other side!"* Once he realized this, he stopped partying on the weekends. He stopped lounging around after work during the week. He buckled up, got out his tools, finished the job, and got that place livable. He put an ad up on Craigslist and had tenants in there two weeks later.

The reason he was unmotivated was he did not understand the concept of opportunity cost. He didn't think of the rent he was losing as his. But it was his. In a very real sense, he was throwing a very attainable $1000 per month down the drain simply by refusing to do the simple actions necessary to collect it.

When there is money readily available for the taking, do what is necessary to collect it! Do not leave money on the table that's yours to collect.

Failing to Invest

Investors always have to make choices about whether to invest their money and time. And an obvious consequence of choosing to invest in one thing means the investor can't simultaneously invest that money in something else.

> *Janet had $10,000 in 1980 and was torn between the choice of investing in Apple stock, or stuffing the money in her mattress. Because it was a "safer" investment, Janet chose to hide the money in her mattress, and decades later, that money is still there, safe and sound. Meanwhile, Jack used his $10,000 to purchase Apple computer stock, also in 1980. Today, Jack is a multimillionaire.*

Okay, this is an extreme example. Everyone wishes they had invested in Apple way back when. But in this too-simplistic example, we see opportunity cost at play. Janet had the opportunity to invest in Apple, but chose instead not to invest, for fear of losing her hard-earned cash. While she didn't lose her money, she missed out on the extraordinary opportunity offered by that particular investment. In a very real sense, Janet's decision to not invest in Apple Computers cost her millions of dollars.

Investing Suboptimally and the Cost of Capital

Investors are faced with opportunity cost dilemmas at all times and must accept a simple fact: It is impossible to bet big on every stock, every property, and every business opportunity that has great potential. No one gets every investment right, every time. Yet, each time that "wrong" investment is chosen, the investor loses not only the money invested, but also all the money they could have made in a more successful investment.

While it's impossible to choose the most successful investment possible every time, investors can measure the success of their approach over the long term. To do this, investors can compare their results to what the average investor gets over a similar time period. This brings up another question: *What are "average" returns, and how does one go about getting "average" returns?* There are many different numbers that folks in the finance world throw out at this point.

For the purposes of this discussion, you should assume that the average investor achieves returns of at least 10 percent per year. Therefore, you should invest in such a manner as to *consistently achieve significantly* greater returns than 10 percent per year on your money. Here are three reasons why

10 percent is a reasonable investment threshold to shoot for:

First, over the period from 1928 to 2015, the geometric mean return of the S&P 500 was 9.5 percent, which is very close to this 10 percent return rate. As it's possible to invest in index funds (an activity that requires essentially no effort) that closely match the returns of the S&P 500, it makes no sense to expend effort to attain returns that are not significantly greater than those that can be had without doing much of anything!

Second, 10 percent is a reasonably high return. Most loans to reputable people and businesses will carry interest rates and returns lower than 10 percent. Consistently getting a greater than 10 percent return will require some thought and effort, and likely a bit of personal touch. It will force investors to get mildly creative.

Third, 10 percent is an easy number to work with. When investing $22,000, any investor can easily calculate that they need to produce at least $2200 per year on their money to achieve a return that meets a 10 percent return expectation. Easy math allows the investor to screen potential investments quickly.

In the language of finance, 10 percent per year is our cost of capital. If we assume that we could earn 10 percent returns on $10,000, then the cost of capital (the cost of failing to invest) is $1000 per year.

Here are some takeaways from the discussion of opportunity cost:

- There is a very real cost to *not* taking action.

- There is a very real cost to *not* investing our available excess funds.

- The cost of an investment that loses money is *greater* than just the money lost, since all the returns that *could* have been achieved in another investment are lost as well!

- There is no way to be right *all* the time, with every investment decision, so investors have to choose an acceptable level of success, something greater than a return, but less than the best possible return.

- You need a reasonable target to shoot for when assessing investment returns. A reasonable target to shoot for is significantly greater returns than 10 percent, which approximates the long-term average return of the US equity marketplace.

- If an investor isn't confident or interested in acquiring the knowledge or putting in the effort to achieve significantly higher returns than 10 percent, they might as well just invest in stock index funds, and focus on earning more and saving more instead of on managing their investments.

Diversification and Risk Management

Diversification is an interesting concept, because it's typically used as a way to "reduce risk." However, in this book, risk isn't defined as probability of a loss in value in the short-term, but as the probability of an investment producing less long-term wealth than another investment or set of investments. Given the goal of early financial freedom, the concept of diversification, as many traditional financial advisors define it, doesn't apply. Let's illustrate an example of traditional diversification.

Joe is worth exactly $1M dollars. His net worth is divided as follows:

- $250,000 is in real estate equity

- $250,000 is in stocks

- $250,000 is in bonds

- $250,000 is in cash

In this example, Joe is diversified, with his wealth split evenly among four asset classes. Joe's financial planner tells him that he is "protected from a downturn" or that he "has exposure to multiple asset classes." These are true statements. Joe has $1M, and it's unlikely that he will lose all or even most of his wealth in the event of a market crash in one or more of these asset classes. For example, if stocks lose half their value ($125,000 in his case), Joe will still have $875,000 in net worth. If he had not diversified, and had his entire $1M dollars invested in stocks, he would have lost $500,000 in value.

It is the fear of losing a huge proportion of their paper wealth that leads most folks with significant assets to diversify. However, the rational investor holding wealth of under a few hundred thousand dollars should not manage assets so as to mitigate the risk of loss. She should conclude, instead, that the ideal way to manage assets is to focus exclusively on that asset class she feels is likely to produce the largest and most accessible long-term returns, and to invest in that asset class consistently until the desired amount of wealth is accumulated. The goal in this book is to rapidly attain a state of financial freedom as early in life as possible, not to preserve a small amount of wealth.

There are two primary reasons why investors of the circumstances and type that this book is written for should invest in the asset classes with the greatest statistical probability of creating wealth, rather than diversifying away their risk:

First, diversification assumes that protection of principal is the most important goal. While protection of principal is important, remember that as investors, we abide first and foremost by Tenet #1: Investors never spend the principal.

Protection of the principal isn't the most important goal, especially for someone just getting started in a career or in building wealth. Rapid accumulation and expansion of capital, within reasonable limits, is far more important, given the goals of readers of this book. It is almost certainly much more efficient to build net worth, for example, by house hacking (discussed in chapter 4) for a few years than to try to build up an equivalent equity position in stocks. However, that strategy will inevitably result in a portfolio mostly comprised of real estate.

Is the investor wrong to have all her wealth in real estate by pursuing this strategy? Is he at risk? Perhaps so. But, the key distinction is that by investing in the most advantaged asset class, that person *has a reasonable chance to build significant wealth into the hundreds of thousands of dollars, worth protecting via diversification,* unlike someone just getting started with their $25,000 portfolio allocated carefully among various index and bond funds.

Who would you rather be: The guy with $500,000 that's at risk of losing a big piece of that wealth due to lack of diversification? Or, the guy with $50,000 that's well protected? Spreading out all of your wealth into many different types of investments obviously means that you are less likely to lose it all, but you are also *protecting yourself from upside.*

Diversification is extremely important to certain investors: The very wealthy and those near retirement in particular.

Jimmy is sixty-four years old, and has built up a $750,000 retirement account. He is hoping to withdraw $50,000 per year, or about 6.7 percent per year. If the portfolio gets wiped out by a stock market crash and loses 50 percent of its value, Jimmy is screwed. If he needs that $50,000 per year to survive, he is highly likely to run out of money in the next few years, and he is too old to return to high paying work. For Jimmy, diversification into safe investments that are highly likely to retain their value makes sense.

Jimmy might be wise to spread his wealth around into relatively safe bonds and other very safe debt, with a small amount in other asset classes like stocks and real estate. However, the cost of this safety is that Jimmy is likely to achieve returns of just a few percentage points— maybe 3 to 4 percent yields per year on a conservative bond portfolio. A young investor aspiring to early financial freedom may feel that this approach makes little sense. Yes, the young investor might see large price fluctuations in his stock holdings over the short term. But, over a fifty-year investment timeframe, he is much more likely to achieve approximately 10 percent annual returns on his initial capital by investing 100 percent in index funds than by investing half in stocks and half in lower-yielding bonds.

The second reason why diversification, in a traditional sense, may not apply to the reader of this book is that the reader of this book is developing a holistic life position that actually *welcomes* the possibility of a market crash. This can be explained with a concept called *dollar cost averaging*.

Folks are always afraid that they are investing at the very peak of the market, such that their investments might drop in value in the imminent crash. In other words, they think that they are going to invest at the peak points of this graph.

Value of $100 - Stocks Vs T-Bonds

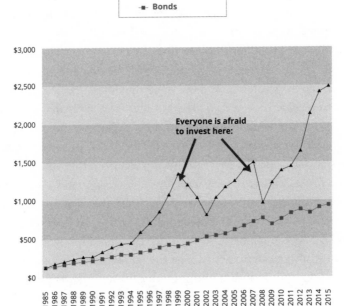

The problem is almost no one will experience an outcome even remotely close to that, assuming they intend to keep their initial capital invested forever, and assuming they invest all excess cash flow in their life consistently throughout their life. Think about it. If you haven't completed part I and II of this book, do you have $50,000 right now, sitting in your bank account, ready to be invested? Likely not. You probably have much less than that, and plan to accumulate or invest a few hundred dollars or a few thousand dollars per month at first, and to consistently add anything you can to your portfolio as you earn it and save it!

The reason why stock market crashes are nothing to fear can, perhaps, be best explained through the concept of dollar cost averaging mentioned earlier. Dollar cost averaging is the practice of consistently buying a fixed amount of an investment over time. For example, if you plan to purchase $1000 of an index fund each month for many years, you would be dollar cost averaging. This is a common way to invest, because many people simply contribute a little bit to their investment portfolio every month or every couple of weeks when they get paid or otherwise have a little extra cash.

Suppose Becky wants to retire in ten years. For the next five years, the market climbs. In years six and seven, there is a big crash, and the market climbs again. Assuming Becky invested throughout this period in regular increments as she receives a paycheck, she will have navigated the crash successfully, because she bought before the crash, during the crash, and after the crash! She was consistent. Sure, her investments right before the crash dropped in value, but her investments during the crash have recovered nicely and made up for much of the loss. This is how to navigate a crash!

In real life, of course, you are going to be saving as much as you can, earning as much as you can, and investing the difference, so your contributions won't be exactly even each month. But, if you apply that principle and invest as much as you can reasonably afford with each passing paycheck, then you are likely to reasonably replicate the results of dollar-cost-averaging, and sustain a near average rate of return for the securities that you invest in.

This means you can stick with one asset class, and be comfortable with your choice, because you know that over the next few decades you will sometimes buy high, and sometimes buy low. And who cares if you start today and the market is about to crash? The objective is to sustain a system of wealth creation, not to time the markets perfectly. As long as you consistently purchase an asset class that's capable of sustaining long-term returns and are comfortable with your choice, you are likely to build wealth regardless of market highs and lows.

Investors with the goal and investment philosophy outlined in this book don't need to worry about short-term volatility, even extreme volatility. They don't need to worry because they are working toward financial freedom and are not yet dependent on their assets for income to sustain their lifestyle. They don't need to worry because they are building in a margin of error by accumulating such a large amount of assets with returns that exceed that of their spending. And, they don't need to worry because if the market crashes and their current investments lose value, they will be presented with the opportunity to buy additional assets at a low cost.

Investors subscribing to this philosophy are rewarded with a win-win scenario. If one is investing in stocks, and stocks go up, then great news! The investor has made some money and increased her net worth. If stocks go down, then this is also great news! The investor gets to purchase stocks at a lower price than he could the day before, and therefore will be better off than if stocks had risen prior to the next investment.

Wrapping Up Diversification

The point of building wealth is to increase the number of options in your life, and to achieve a state of incredible opportunity and choice early in life. If you are going to be working toward this goal for the next few years, you might as well pursue the investments that are likely to produce long-term sustainable wealth, even if that comes at the cost of short-term volatility. So, while a typical financial planner is correct in saying that a diversified portfolio protects the investor from any downturns, it also *prevents the investor from benefitting fully from the performance of stronger asset classes!*

Two additional points on diversification: First, diversification within an asset class is very wise. Take stocks for example. It is unacceptably risky to put one's entire net worth into stock in a single company. Individual companies decline or bankrupt all the time, and the investor's life savings are at risk in their entirety. Instead, you can purchase something called an *index fund*, a fund that buys many stocks of companies around the country and the world. While any one company may lose all or nearly all its value, it would be absurd to think that all of the major companies on the planet (or even in a country) will lose all or nearly all of their value. This is smart diversification. Index fund investing will be explained in detail in the next chapter.

Second, diversification can become a useful tool as your wealth grows and as you accumulate significant assets to protect. Those on the brink of retirement, those who plan never to work again, those who want to be as sure as possible that their money will last as long as possible, and those who want to set aside money to provide for their family with a high degree of certainty should all diversify. An asset allocation like Joe's mentioned earlier ($1 million net worth, with $250,000 in each of real estate, stocks, bonds, and cash) might not be a bad plan if you planned to retire for the rest of your life on that and wanted to sleep peacefully at night. Contrast this with a fledgling investor with 1 percent of Joe's wealth ($10,000) with $10,000 spread across stocks bonds, and real estate. This fledgling investor protects his $10,000, sure, but he also ensures he goes nowhere fast.

There is plenty of time to diversify once you have a net worth exceeding $100,000, $200,000, $500,000, or even $1,000,000. But, if your goal is to give yourself the best odds at achieving financial freedom early in life, diversifying your first $25,000 in stocks, bonds, gold, and whatever else is unlikely get you there quickly.

Passive Income

Passive income is a misnomer in that it implies that income is received passively—without the need for *any* effort. Most investors won't have such an experience at significant scale. Instead of seeking totally passive income, investors should seek investments that produce large amounts of income with relatively little work. They should look for opportunities to solve problems in return for large savings or revenue opportunities. I can explain this through a personal example. While real estate is by no means totally passive, it's certainly takes a high paying job to take care of problems related to my properties. One of my duplexes brings in $2625 per month. If I were to hire a property management company, this duplex might cost me $265.50 per month (10 percent of the rents) to manage. Instead, when tenants give me a call about a problem with the property, I simply take that call myself, and give the handyman, plumber, or electrician a call.

In this case, property management doesn't actually *do* any of the work on the property, other than paperwork, and making sure the tenants pay rent on time—for all of the handyman and repair work, they just hire it out for me. In another example, when some squirrels were running around the roof of my rental property, my tenants informed me of the problem. I then called the pest control folks and got a quote for $2000 for a three-hour operation. Two thousand dollars is a tremendous amount of money to patch a few holes ($120 in materials) and install a $60 squirrel trap. Instead of paying this ridiculous amount of money, I told the squirrel people to buzz off and did the work myself in about three hours.

Doing the work myself cost me less than $200 at Home Depot, and took three hours out of my Saturday afternoon. Is that truly passive income? Maybe not. But when's the last time you made $600 per hour?

Don't think you can sit back and collect passive income without doing any work. Managing wealth will be a lifelong pursuit. Even if you outgrow active involvement of your assets, businesses, or properties, you will still be managing the managers of your assets. It will never be truly passive in the sense that you will never have to track or think about your wealth at all. Don't shy away from monthly cash flows that take a little bit of effort to maintain, and instead view them as exceptionally high wage jobs that require a small amount of effort periodically.

Materiality versus Return on Investment

Have you ever heard someone brag about making $1000 on a stock purchase? It's pathetic. Folks make $80,000+ per year, with degrees from top business schools, and yet go on about their $1000 win on Facebook stock. What these folks fail to realize is that there are two keys to investment returns. The two keys are the percentage return on investment, and the materiality of the investment.

The definition of materiality that applies here is "the quality of being relevant or significant," Let's use an example to flesh out this definition.

> *Suppose Evan goes out to Costco and spends $50 to purchase 100 plastic water bottles, a bag or two of ice, and a cooler. Suppose he then goes right next to the ballpark, and sells these water bottles for $1 apiece, dodging the police or stadium security. By the end of the game, he might have made $100, or a 200 percent return on investment (ROI).*

Evan has two choices at this time:

1. He can brag about how incredible his return was.

2. He can realize that he is working basically a minimum wage job and do something that actually matters for his financial position.

The obvious reason you don't go out and purchase water bottles to sell outside the ballpark is that the return on this investment is so small it isn't worth your time. Or, in other words, that kind of return is immaterial, given the size of the investment and the work that went into it.

Most people accept this fact, and don't sell water bottles outside of sports stadiums as a result, except for low earners, or the unemployed—for them it might be worth their time. However, middle-class Americans attempting to begin investing fail to take this line of thinking to the next logical step, insofar as money management goes.

They fail to see how this applies to other endeavors, like stock investing. Stock picking is a waste of time, especially for a young person with low starting net worth. Spending hours and hours picking stocks is the full-time employee's equivalent of selling water bottles outside the stadium. It is a low wage, low-reward task that rarely produces big winners. Young investors with little net worth are extremely unlikely to produce outsized returns by trading in the public markets. Even if a young prodigy *could* produce incredible returns (like Warren Buffet), this prodigy would be wasting their time picking stocks at a low level of net worth. We cover this topic more fully in the next chapter.

Alternative Investments

In the next chapters, we will discuss investing in stocks and real estate in depth as it relates to attaining the goal of early financial freedom. Unfortunately, this book will not spend more than a cursory amount of time discussing the countless other types of investing available. Just because they are not discussed here, doesn't mean that there aren't other viable approaches to investing and building real assets that help you attain early financial freedom. Many people who attained early financial freedom or built significant wealth at an early age did so by taking advantage of unique circumstances or opportunities.

If you are truly passionate or committed to attaining early financial freedom so quickly that real estate investing and index fund investing are simply too slow, then you will need to find means of investing that are more aggressive and more suited to your personal situation.

Here are some examples of other ways that individuals have built wealth and achieved early financial freedom:

- Invest with options

- Create or buy a blog

- Buy a small business

- Write a book
- Lend with peer-to-peer lending
- Create YouTube videos
- Become an angel investor
- Rent out a home out through Airbnb
- Build an app
- Build an online course
- Gamble (no, this isn't recommended)
- Become an Internet entrepreneur

Any of these strategies could work for a specific individual. Some are likely to be slower than index fund investing, but with more cash flow (like peer-to-peer lending), and others have the potential to build incredible wealth rapidly (like becoming an Internet entrepreneur). Others offer a low probability of success but great excitement along the way (like gambling).

Opportunities to build, buy, or create assets through the means above and many others will multiply for you as you progress toward early financial freedom and extend your financial runway. While there isn't time to discuss every viable investing approach in this book, understand that countless opportunities will materialize for you throughout your life. You have only to reach out and seize them! The further you progress toward financial freedom, the more opportunities you will be able to access and the more resources you will be able to deploy to capitalize on them.

In the next two chapters, the two types of investing that will be discussed are index fund investing and real estate investing. There's no reason you can't experiment with other approaches if you prefer or want to try your hand at something new. And, if index fund investing is too slow, and real estate investing is too much work or not right for your circumstances, you need to acquire the tools or skills necessary to pursue another strategy. If that's the case, good luck to you—and let the rest of us know how you get there.

Conclusion

Investing is challenging, engaging, rewarding, and fun. Investing is an area of wealth management that will require lifelong study and constant attention. Those who achieve financial freedom at an early age will spend most of their lives managing their assets and investments, rather than working to earn a wage. Achieving excellent investment returns will require constant attention throughout one's life, but can produce wealth well in excess of that which can be earned through wages or saved through frugal living.

However, it's inefficient and dangerous to attempt to generate significant investment returns (greater than $10,000 per year) without the personal financial pieces in place. A young investor with less than $100,000 to invest is unlikely to generate a return that will materially hasten his journey to early financial freedom, and therefore should focus his efforts on accumulating assets of a material nature with which to invest.

Additionally, while still in the asset accumulation phase, diversification makes little sense for the seeker of early financial freedom. Diversification reduces both the risk and potential reward to be gained from investing in any one specific asset class. Those with significant holdings who are no longer interested in or able to earn income and accumulate assets benefit from diversification and the protection of their current levels of wealth. But, the seeker of early financial freedom simply diversifies away his chance at rapid wealth growth if he diversifies his holdings.

Understand risk. Risk is the probability of having less wealth over time. A portfolio comprised of bonds bearing little interest is highly likely to produce little wealth compared with a portfolio comprised of stocks. History tells us that the owner of stocks is likely to become far wealthier over time than the owner of bonds. Invest in an asset class that you believe will help you to produce above-average investment returns.

Throughout your journey, abide by the seven core tenets of investing. Apply your knowledge and effort to investments that you can control and in which you personally are able to produce a competitive advantage. *Never* spend the principal, *reinvest* the majority of your investment returns, and build wealth forever.

The informed investor, who develops a sound philosophy, will reap the rewards of this study in increasing amounts throughout her life. Understand why concepts that apply to Average Joe may not apply to you. Invest like the wealthy. Generate passive income, and invest for growth. Challenge yourself to seek far superior returns to the 10 percent generated by the stock market. If you don't think you can attain that return, consider investing in index funds which historically approach that return rate. Or, focus on something creative that synergizes heavily with your work or lifestyle. There are lots of choices; don't be timid about exploring them. And be proactive in your quest for early financial freedom.

Chapter 10
Investing in the Stock Market

As touched on briefly in the last chapter, index fund investing is a great way to have a good statistical chance of matching the historical returns of the stock market. It also ensures that your returns will be no better than the historical return of equity markets. While average returns will not speed you on your way to early financial freedom, the fact that average returns can be achieved with essentially *no effort* will enable you to apply your efforts elsewhere in pursuit of earning more money or designing an ever more efficient lifestyle.

When one invests in stock, they are buying a portion of a company. For example, when Jack purchases a share of Apple stock, he owns a tiny fraction of the company. Apple was among the best investments in the past century for early shareholders. Investors that bought and held stock in Apple back in the seventies and eighties are now well-documented millionaires.

However, for every Apple, there are many more publicly traded companies that didn't make it big, and a number that eventually went bankrupt. Investors who purchase stock in those companies often lose all or most of their investment.

Investing in just one company is a highly risky proposition as it produces an unacceptably high probability of losing all of the investment with no hope for recovery. One way to reduce the odds of losing money involves purchasing the stock of several companies. Suppose, for example, that an investor owned the following companies in even amounts:

- Apple
- Alphabet (the parent company of Google)
- Microsoft

- Amazon

- Berkshire Hathaway

- Exxon Mobil

- Facebook

- Johnson & Johnson

- General Electric

- Wells Fargo

The owner of this portfolio is unlikely to lose all of his investment quickly. These are all large, stable companies unlikely to all go bankrupt anytime soon. Even if one of them *does* lose a lot of money, the other nine may grow or hold steady and therefore make up for any losses.

This kind of diversification is smart. This kind of diversification protects investors from events that are outside of their control, but still allow them to take advantage of the market as a whole. Remember, stocks tend to produce returns in the ballpark of 10 percent compounded annually, so diversifying in such a manner as to be exposed to that kind of long term appreciation makes sense.

Do Not Attempt to Pick Individual Stocks

A savvy reader might point out that buying the ten companies mentioned just above reduces the impact any one particularly fast-growing company might have on their portfolio. They might argue that if they were to put all of their money only into the company they believe is most likely to grow quickly in the next few years, they will become far wealthier far faster. Almost everyone who studies investing jumps to this conclusion at first. It makes sense. *Obviously*, Apple was a good bet! Why can't we pick the next company like Apple?

The answer to that question is rather lengthy. Read on below to understand the two major reasons why attempting to invest in individual stocks is likely to be a waste of time that produces no excess wealth for the average investor with little to no starting wealth.

Reason #1: The Competition Is Out of Your League

One of the reasons that attempting to pick individual winning stocks is so difficult is many other investors are also trying to do exactly that. There is an entire industry of folks who manage other people's money. These people attempt to pick winning stocks, companies that are likely to grow in value faster than the market. They are often highly paid, have excellent access to information and company management, and have years of experience in their markets.

Let me introduce you to Matt. Matt is an investment banker who does equity research in the energy markets—oil and gas companies. He spends perhaps eighty hours each week studying his industry, and has done this for over a decade. He reads annual reports, market news, and press releases from his Bloomberg terminal, and studies investor decks the moment they become available.

He also attends annual shareholder meetings, networks directly with executive officers at the Fortune 500 companies he invests in, and meets with other large stakeholders from all over the country. Matt is one of the most well informed pros in his entire industry and is therefore in, perhaps, the best position imaginable to predict the future success or failure of these companies.

After hundreds of hours of careful research and methodical number crunching, Matt leverages his research and his decade of experience to purchase, or recommend the purchase, of tens of millions or hundreds of millions of dollars in equity in the companies he researches. He also knows when to dump companies.

Matt is every bit as smart as you, and as an alumnus of an elite business school, he is better educated than you. He's willing to work 80 hours per week and to do everything in his power to get access to critical information the moment it becomes available. He studies the market all day long and goes home to dream about it at night. He is training young analysts (also smarter, better-educated, and working longer hours than you) in his approach to perform ever more thorough due diligence. Because of his training, expertise, resources, and results, thousands of wealthy investors give Matt money to invest, or invest on their own on the basis of his recommendations.

Matt's fund has well over $500 million in assets under management. He buys and sells enough shares of multi-billion dollar companies that he can single-handedly change their market price with individual transactions or market recommendations.

Because of his efforts, resources, training, and expertise, Matt has beaten the market by about 1 to 2 percent per year throughout his history as an analyst. He charges high fees for this extraordinary performance, and his happy investors end up slightly better off than if they'd invested in a passive fund investing in technology stocks. They are lucky to invest with Matt because 85 percent of his competitors failed to beat their benchmark last year, after fees.

Guys like Matt move the majority of the money in the market. You aren't competing with other people like you, who are investing in stocks part time while making a living from a day job. You are competing with Matt. Matt moves tens or hundreds of millions of dollars into and out of companies. Average investors move hundreds or thousands of dollars into and out of companies.

You will have to get up very early in the morning to match Matt's performance, just in his sector, with your own stock picking, in your spare time. Best of luck to you.

Reason #2: The Alpha Isn't Worth It

Ok, so you think Matt doesn't exist. He's a fairy tale ogre invented to scare you. Even if he does exist, you can beat him. The other books and blog posts, and your Uncle Jimmy, tell you Matt is actually too informed, too smart, and too big. You're better than him. You get what the little guy is doing; you see the stuff on the ground that the Wall Street guys can't, or won't. You are a prodigy.

Even if you are a stock-picking prodigy—the greatest of all time—it's only worthwhile to devote serious effort toward beating the market if you have hundreds of thousands, or maybe millions to invest. Ninety-nine percent of the readers of this book won't have that amount of capital, even after the completion of parts I and II. Without a meaningful amount of capital, chasing above-market returns is as silly as selling bottled water outside the ballpark to generate "returns" you can brag about.

David decided to try his hand at picking stocks back in early 2014 when he had saved his first nifty $5000. He spent hours reading annual reports of so-called "micro-caps" (companies with less than $100 million in market value). He read annual reports, got in touch with key executives, called up stores that sold or used their products, and performed all other types of crazy due diligence.

And guess what? In 2014, a year when the S&P shot up 11.4 percent, he managed to *lose* money. There are three possibilities as to why he lost: He's either really unlucky, really dumb, or stock picking is just really, really, hard. It's probably all three.

Let's suppose things had gone differently. Let's suppose he was a stock-picking prodigy like Matt or a legendary investor capable of sustaining long-term returns like Warren Buffet. Let's suppose that instead of losing money, he earned a 25 percent return on his $5000 investment and brought home a cool $1250 in 2014. Let's also suppose that he was able to produce this incredible result, beating full-time investors like Matt and legendary greats like Buffet on just ten hours of research per week in his spare time.

In this scenario, he would have beaten the market's return of 11.4 percent by 13.6 percent. That additional 13.6 percent return (which again, is *extraordinary* as an investing achievement) is what investors like to call *alpha*—here defined as the return you generate in excess of the market average. On a $5000 investment, David's *alpha* in this scenario equates to just $680. Over 500 hours (fifty weeks at ten hours per week in this example) of research went into that alpha. That's roughly $1.36 per hour.

Selling water bottles outside the stadium is starting to look a little better, huh? David could easily make all that money in just five to ten games, and perhaps fifteen to thirty total hours of work! The point is that you might *feel* like a badass for getting that 25 percent return, but the reality is very far from badass. In this scenario, David would have been much better off working even a minimum wage job, building a passive asset, or focusing on saving more money. Picking stocks was an utter waste of time from a profitability standpoint. In fact, David got hosed, even though he produced an extraordinary investment return! Even if he'd produced this extraordinary result with a $50,000 initial investment, his returns in this scenario equate to just $13.60 per hour!

Realistically, the best of the best only dare to hope for 1 to 2 percent above-market returns over the long run. In order to earn a median salary of $50,000 per year, you'd need to have $2.5M to $5M in the bank to justify putting in a real full-time effort to pick stocks. And if you are picking them in your free time? Well, best of luck.

For some reason, this is the activity that folks associate with investing. It should not be. So why do people pick stocks? It's because they are *lazy*. Picking stocks is something easy that would-be investors can do over the Internet with just a few thousand dollars. Investors can read a few books and pretend to themselves that they know what they are doing, and it can *feel* like they are doing really well when they watch some of their picks go up, even though others may fall.

Picking stocks is something you can put a ton of time into, talk about, sound smart with other people, and do in a free moment at work, or from your couch. They are easy to check, track, and chart, and they are something to discuss with coworkers, friends, and family.

The trouble with it all, however, is that as individuals have proven, picking winning stocks *can be done*. It's just a game where the odds of winning are stacked against you, where more variables than you can count are in play, and where knowledge and hard work often has no bearing on one's success. That's a fool's game.

If, in spite of all of this, you *still* decide to do your own research and individually select stocks to invest in, for goodness sake, don't go in halfway. Go in knowing just how difficult it is, and with the willingness to put in the hours and education, knowing full well that the odds of outperforming the market are against you.

Index Funds Explained

If you invest in stocks, invest with index funds. One example of an index fund is the Vanguard 500 Index Fund (Ticker Symbol VOO). This fund buys a stock in each of the companies in the Standard & Poor's (S&P) 500, and like most index funds, it's a *weighted* fund. This means that if a company is growing fast, it's larger market value is reflected by increasing weight in the investor's portfolio, and companies that are declining become smaller and smaller pieces of the portfolio.

Technical Concept: Ticker Symbols. A ticker symbol is an abbreviation for a stock or fund that you can invest in. In the practical section below, we will demonstrate how to actually purchase your first investment. Actually buying the first investment will involve searching for a stock or fund by its ticker symbol, then buying shares.

Technical Concept: Weighted Average. Suppose that Sean invests $1000 in two companies, with $500 in company A, and $500 in company B. Sean's portfolio is 50 percent company A and 50 percent company B. Later, company A goes up, and company B falls. Sean's portfolio is now comprised of $750 in company A, and $250 in company B. Sean's portfolio, still $1000 in total, is now weighted differently, with 75 percent in company A, and 25 percent in *company B. When the portfolio is comprised of hundreds or thousands of stocks, this math works exactly the same, but spread across more companies.*

This gives the investor three advantages that help him to be successful. First, it ensures that the collapse of one company cannot wipe out an entire portfolio. Second, it exposes the investor to many different companies, enabling the fast growing ones to contribute to their portfolio with increasing weight. Third, and very important, the costs of running index funds are cheap, and as a result index funds have lower fees than actively managed mutual funds.

Many funds out there have fund managers (like Matt, our stock picker from earlier) that try to find stocks that will go up faster than the rest of the market. In spite of copious amounts of research and data that clearly suggest that investing in actively managed funds is likely to produce worse returns than investing in index funds, millions of people still invest in actively managed mutual funds.

Technical Concept: Actively Managed Funds. In an actively managed fund, a fund manager will raise a bunch of money and attempt to pick stocks that do better than other stocks in the market. These fund managers will often charge a fee for their services. For example, a "growth fund" manager might raise $100M from thousands of small investors, and attempt to pick some tech companies that will shoot up in value. In exchange, investors might pay him with 1 percent of their investment each year, in this case, $1 million per year. As we've shown earlier, almost no one can pick stocks that consistently beat the market over the long term, and even if they did beat the market by 0.5 percent or so, the extra value they provide is reduced by their expensive 1 percent fee for fund management. Trying to find a fund manager who can beat the other fund managers' investing performance over many years is perhaps even more difficult than trying to pick stocks that will go up faster than the market average. It's just not a strategy that has any statistical evidence of success. Index funds, by contrast, often charge tiny fees—in the ballpark of 0.05 to 0.07 percent for exceptionally low cost popular ones like Vanguard and Fidelity. These fees are as small as they can reasonably be. It is these low fees that give index fund investors a great opportunity to achieve returns that closely mirror the market as a whole.

Technical Concept: S&P 500. The S&P 500 is a composite of some of the largest 500 stocks that represent the US equity market. Many investors like to invest in the stocks in the S&P 500 because they think that investing in big US businesses has been a winning formula for over 100 years.

Index fund investing may be the simplest and most accessible way for new investors to deploy their excess cash in an intelligent manner.

How to Invest in an Index Fund

To invest in an index fund, visit a large, low-cost investment house or broker, such as Fidelity, Scottrade, E*TRADE, or Vanguard. Another viable choice is Robinhood, a mobile app that allows investors to trade stocks for free. Once logged in, these companies will provide instruction to help you set up a brokerage account, connect your bank account, and transfer the money you would like to invest to your new brokerage account. Make sure to do your own research on index funds and pick one or several that represent reasonable, large chunks of the economy. Then follow the instructions on the brokerage or investment management company's website or app to purchase shares of the index fund. Remember, you will need to know the ticker symbol of the stock or fund that you want to buy, and the number of shares or dollars that you wish to invest. If you are investing $1000, for example, and shares are priced at $100, then you would purchase ten shares.

Conclusion

Investing in the stock market, and more specifically, in index funds, will not make you rich quickly. But, an average result can be obtained with *little to no effort*. The fact that this type of asset accumulation is so mindless and so effortless is its advantage. If you pursue this path, understand that the only way you will hasten early financial freedom is by continually increasing the difference between your earned income and your spending. You will have to continually earn more money and spend little money to eventually reach a point where stock investments can deliver early financial freedom at a conservative safe withdrawal rate.

While there are exceptions to every rule, the fact of the matter is that the vast majority of investors who seek to earn outsized stock market returns by performing security analysis are likely to underperform the average return produced by market index funds. The same is true for attempting to select a fund *manager* to manage their money for them. There are just very few individuals who will achieve lasting success investing in the stock market over and above the returns produced by index funds.

If you can average $25,000 per year in savings, outside of investment returns, you might be able to achieve early financial freedom (~$500,000) in twelve years with this strategy. Eight, if you can up that to $50,000 per year in savings. If you pursue this investment strategy as the primary means through which you accumulate assets, understand that you will need to focus your efforts heavily in the areas of income production and spending to achieve your goals.

Chapter 11
Real Estate Investing

Chapter 4 went into great detail about purchasing a primary residence, and demonstrating the financial impact of house hacking—that is, buying an investment property to be also used as a primary residence. Renting out additional units or rooms in a house can turn it into an asset and produce incredible financial gains. Given the extraordinary advantages of buying a primary residence in this manner, it's logical to presume that the strategy can be repeated over and over again with similar results.

This approach can be an efficient way to build wealth rapidly, as a hobby on the side, in a way that's minimally invasive to the investor's free time. Many people have simply house hacked their way, one property at a time, to early financial freedom. It offers the investor the ability to synergize their investing strategy with their lifestyle, and it offers the investor a strategy that allows for personal touch and effort to contribute to the investment.

Regardless of how you acquire rental properties, they are an excellent wealth building tool for folks looking to generate stronger overall returns than the stock market, at the cost of a short learning curve and likely a significant amount of time selecting and managing them. Here are five reasons why real estate investing is an excellent investment approach for those seeking early financial freedom:

Five Reasons to Invest in Real Estate
Reason #1: Rental Properties Build Wealth in Multiple Ways
Rental properties help investors build wealth in three ways:
   1. Income

2. Appreciation

3. Loan Amortization

Rental properties produce income in the form of rent. Assuming the investor does his homework and buys correctly, the investor can produce rent in excess of the mortgage payment, taxes, insurance, repairs, maintenance, and the other costs associated with owning a rental property. The excess cash flow can then be used to fund early financial freedom, or saved to be reinvested in the purchase of additional rental properties or other income producing assets.

Rental properties can also appreciate when home values go up or when they are improved. An investor can look for deals that are undervalued or in an up and coming area to get a shot at excellent appreciation. This kind of speculation may be a great idea for investors looking to take advantage of trends in their local market, so long as the property is an income-appreciating asset regardless of whether the local market improves. Furthermore, the investor can capture still more value by improving the property by fixing it up, or managing the process of fixing it up. This can increase rents, or increase the value of the property.

Finally, rental properties are often purchased with debt financing. Each month, tenants pay rent and that rent is used to pay down a loan on the property. That loan pay down results in more equity for the owner, and builds wealth in conjunction with the appreciation and income that the property is generating.

These advantages to rental property investing are further compounded by special tax advantages that real estate investors enjoy. For example, phantom expenses like depreciation can offset rental property income. This increases your after-tax cash flow relative to some other types of investments.

Reason #2: Rental Properties Allow the Investor Control

Real estate investors have much more control over their investments than folks who invest in the stock market or with other publicly traded securities. They can find creative ways to reduce expenses, take over when things get out of hand, and mitigate problems.

There are many, many amateur landlords out there operating rentals with little to no experience, and with few systems in place to run an efficient business—meaning that if you treat this business like a business you have a good shot at competing effectively. Countless people have inherited rentals, kept former homes after they've moved out, bought real estate without any prior education, or otherwise gone into landlording without prior preparation.

This offers opportunity to the investor looking to run their rental property business seriously—as opposed to someone who manages a former home they couldn't sell or who inherited a rental. A savvy investor can build a system to deal with problems, fix up the property himself or hire it out as makes sense in his personal situation. There is plenty of opportunity to compete effectively in the marketplace for the investor willing to commit to the business for the long term and put in effort upfront.

Reason #3: Rental Properties Allow the Investor to Benefit from Leverage

Leveraging (buying real estate with a loan) allows the investor to control more property with less money and offers opportunities for smart investors to more rapidly build wealth and move toward financial freedom. With a 20 percent down payment, an investor can purchase a property roughly five times higher value than if they were to buy a property for cash. This has the effect of immediately compounding the rewards and risks of real estate fivefold.

Suppose Lowell has $100,000 and buys a property without a loan (a $100,000 property). If this property appreciates 5 percent after a year, then after one year it will be worth $105K—and Lowell has profited $5000.

If on the other hand, Lowell were to use the $100,000 as a down payment on a property worth $500K, getting a loan for $400,000 in the process, he is using leverage. If the property goes up 5 percent, then it is worth $525K. Lowell profited $25K!

It's possible to compute the effects of leverage by using a financial model. While the model assumes constant returns at market averages, note that as a practical matter, returns tend to be volatile and prices rise and fall over the years in less predictably smooth curves. Regardless, this financial model is useful in terms of looking at how an average investor might plan out his or her strategy over the very long term.

In this analysis, the model looks at a $62,500 property purchased with $12,500 down and a $50,000 loan (leveraged at 4:1). But, the math works with everything from this tiny purchase to real estate valued at millions or hundreds of millions of dollars. Let's look at two graphs produced by this model:

Annual Return on Equity Next 10 Years

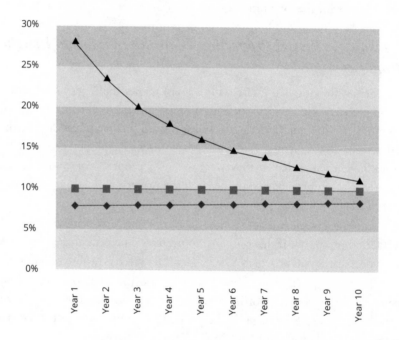

Legend:
- ▲ Leveraged Real Estate
- ■ All-Cash Stocks
- ◆ All-Cash Real Estate

- Notice, first of all that unleveraged real estate (the diamond line) performs worse than the stock market (the square line) over time, on average. Leveraged real estate, on the other hand, typically produces larger returns for investors than the stock market over the first decade, and then produces lower than average returns after that as the portfolio deleverages and the debt is paid down.

Annual Cashflow Next 10 Years

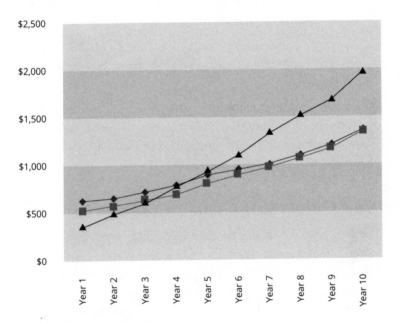

- ▲ **Leveraged Real Estate**
- ■ **All-Cash Stocks**
- ◆ **All-Cash Real Estate**

- Notice, second of all, that leveraged real estate initially produces less cash flow than the dividends typically disbursed by stocks in the S&P 500 index on an equivalent investment. In fact, it's about 3.5 years before a leveraged property will on average generate cash flow in excess of buying property with all cash, or in excess of the dividends disbursed by an index fund.

It's important to note that leveraged real estate investments deleverage with each passing year. As properties deleverage, rents increase, and landlords gain more experience, cash flow increases. It can quickly surpass the cash flow of the unleveraged purchase, even while return on equity decreases.

Real estate investors that use leverage effectively are presented with a good problem after a few years. On the one hand, they are paying off their loans and getting some great passive cash flow from their investments. On the other hand, they'd actually be better off from a return perspective if they just sold their de-leveraging properties and invested in the stock market, or better yet, re-leveraged by selling off their old properties and buying newer, bigger, and better ones! While this is a good problem to have, it's important to always think "What's next?" when designing any investment strategy to save yourself from costly mistakes or inaction down the line. The key points here are these:

1. Leveraged real estate produces greater returns on average than unleveraged real estate.

2. Leveraged real estate produces less initial cash flow than unleveraged real estate or even dividends from the stock market on average.

3. Every year, as you pay down the loan, and as the property appreciates in value, your investments will on average deleverage, decreasing your return on equity, but likely increasing your cash flow.

Reason #4: Real Estate Investors Can Trade Up

Megan bought a duplex for $250,000, using a $240,000 loan and $10,000 down payment (using a low down payment loan as a homeowner) in 2017. She goes to sell this duplex in 2021 for $300,000 (the property increases in value because she spent a lot of time fixing it up while she lived there, and the market improves). If the mortgage on the property at that the time of sale is $225,000, then she will net $75,000 from the sale. If she spent the year saving up all the cash flow from this property, her other rentals, and her job, she might have an extra $75,000 to invest on top of that $75,000 for a total of $150,000 in cash. She could take this $150,000 and use it as the down payment on a $600K property, a property that might go on to produce a proportional result to the duplex over the next few years.

This example illustrates how real estate investors become wealthy over time. Megan bought a relatively small property to get things started with her first $10,000 in savings, and was able to leverage that into $75,000 in just a few years.

Successful investors can sell off deleveraging properties, and buy new, larger ones to generate even more rent and potential appreciation. This cycle can significantly speed returns, and is tax-advantaged if done by a knowledgeable investor with a good CPA and broker.

Reason #5: Real Estate Is Manageable While Working a Full-time Job

Every real estate property purchase involves hard work, discipline, and tests a variety of traits, both in acquisition and management. Some people enjoy that challenge and that's why they build huge portfolios or businesses involving millions of dollars and eighty-hour weeks. They like making big sales, hustling and doing everything in their power to scale their businesses. But that's not for everyone.

Many investors choose to invest in real estate to build passive, massive wealth, on the side, and in their spare time on their path to early financial freedom. They earn income with their full-time jobs, live frugally, and with the proceeds of their savings they invest in real estate almost as a hobby.

One transaction per year can produce life changing financial results in less than ten years, and can be quite manageable for even a busy professional. Furthermore, investors who own a small number of properties have more freedom to sell off property that's unpleasant to manage or just takes too much time.

In fact, over 90 percent of real estate investors get their start while working a different full time job, according to a poll on real estate investing website BiggerPockets.com. This is probably because aspiring investors that have the cash for a down payment typically use the income from their jobs to help them qualify for a loan on their first few properties.

How to Invest in Real Estate

There are many ways to invest in real estate. But, this book suggests that you get your feet wet the old fashioned way. If you've completed parts I and II of this book, you will have $100,000 or more with which to invest and now have the ability to put down 20 percent or more toward a median priced investment property in the majority of cities in the country. For example, a $300,000 property would need a $60,000 down payment. If you've accumulated that kind of cash, you'll not only have enough for the down payment, but you'll also have a substantial amount of wealth left over. This means that you can comfortably handle any repairs and expenses that come up, with cash to spare.

Recognize that real estate investing has bankrupted many people. Usually this is because the investor failed to self-educate and had a poor personal financial position going into real estate. However, millions of Americans own rental property. This isn't an unusual or particularly difficult way to build wealth, if the fundamentals are in place. Real estate investors have but to sustain a few basic principles to give themselves a high probability of success:

- They run frugal lives and businesses, relative to generated income.
- They keep plenty of cash on hand to handle large unexpected repairs and maintenance.
- They buy reasonable properties that will obviously produce cash flow after financing and operational expenses.
- They buy in locations that are desirable or that a reasonable person would expect to become more desirable over time.
- They treat their tenants, and those they do business with, honestly and fairly.
- They act consistently, with a long-term outlook.

An investor that keeps these principles in mind doesn't have to fear a doomsday scenario and is likely to generate significant passive income and property equity with each passing month.

Conclusion

Will this path work for everyone? Of course not. Some real estate investors fail, often due to problems with their financial position or ability to manage the business of real estate successfully. But, real estate investing has proven worthwhile for many who work full-time W2 jobs, who also want to build a scalable and minimally invasive real estate business one step at a time.

Real estate investing works best when investors purchase properties during times when they are well capitalized and in a stable life position. Investors with tens of thousands of dollars in the bank set aside for the next purchase, who are pre-approved or extremely well-qualified for financing, or who have other sources of money ready to go are in excellent position to purchase real estate with good odds for success. Similarly, investors willing to commit plenty of time and energy to learning about the fundamentals of real estate investing and overseeing the process of repairing and renting out their properties have greater odds of success than those too busy to be bothered.

For the right investor, real estate is a sustainable, long-term approach to building wealth with stabilized properties that will scale over time. It's not for the aggressive entrepreneur, the man who is ambitious and hungry and ready to dive 100 percent into rapid wealth accumulation, nor is it for the totally passive investor unwilling to put in some hard work to get a head start in wealth creation.

But it is an excellent approach toward attaining early financial freedom for folks who have completed parts I and II of this book and who are looking to deploy significant assets toward real estate investment.

It's not a stretch to execute this strategy and achieve a 25 percent return on your invested dollars through a combination of rental net income, appreciation, loan amortization and sweat for the first few transactions. Due to the nature of compounding returns, if you are able to achieve a 25 percent annual return on your savings, you might achieve a life changing amount of usable wealth in just five to six years if you can save $50,000 per year. That will be about eight years if you can only save $25,000 per year.

Chapter 12
Tracking Your Progress

People tend to succeed in the long term only at those endeavors on which they focus, and inspect regularly. In order to become successful financially, and otherwise, it's imperative you have an understanding of your results on an ongoing basis, and use that understanding to make changes where applicable. It's important you track and measure your efforts when it comes to time and money.

No one is perfect. Everyone wastes time, and everyone wastes money. The goal isn't to become perfect in how you use money and time, but to continually improve and to ultimately put yourself in position to make daily, meaningful progress toward achieving your biggest goals. If you make daily progress and continually improve, you will lead a happier, healthier, more productive, and wealthier life.

Tracking Your Money

This chapter will teach you how to track your progress toward early financial freedom. The single most important metric in this quest is usable net worth, specifically real assets. The good news is this type of net worth can be tracked fairly easily with some degree of accuracy. With regards to your financial picture, in just a few minutes, you can set up a system to stay up-to-date.

Some people track their net worth in spreadsheets, like Microsoft Excel, or by using pencil and paper. That's fine, and has worked for many years. However, nowadays there are neat software products that can take care of this process nearly automatically. Two Internet products that have emerged as leaders in this industry at the time of this writing are Mint and Personal Capital.

If you're not interested in manually tracking your finances on a regular basis, you should sign up for these services or similar ones. Mint and Personal Capital tie directly to investment accounts, bank accounts, loans, and other financial accounts. They can give you a highly accurate picture of your credit score. They even link to outside sources that can give you an opinion of your car's value (Kelley Blue Book) or the value of any real estate you own (Zillow). Note these opinions of asset value can be drastically different than their market value, so don't rely on them too heavily.

When set up correctly, software like Mint and Personal Capital allow you to see your entire financial position across all your accounts in one place. You know how much you owe, and how much you own. You can spot transactions and trends in seconds, rather than after hours of manually tracking things in a spreadsheet. Mint, for example, will alert you to any unusual activity in your account (large transactions, for example). This kind of oversight will almost certainly help you prevent problems, detect fraud, and avoid repeating mistakes. Keep in mind, neither Mint nor Personal Capital can actually create transactions in your accounts, only review, graph, and chart them. They are secure pieces of software backed by large well-known corporations.

If you choose not to link your accounts to Mint and/or Personal Capital, this section should still be valuable for you. Just note that you will have to slightly tweak things and put in more legwork to maintain a clear picture of your financial position. Regardless of how you do it, it's imperative that you track your net worth and each of your individual transactions. You need to collect this data to gain a clear picture of your spending patterns over time. Let's talk what numbers you should track.

The First Financial Metric: Net Worth

One's net worth is simply the number of assets one owns, minus the debts one owes. Folks track net worth in a variety of ways, and have a variety of theories about the best way to do this. Here's a common example of how a typical American might track his net worth:

Sam has the following assets to his name:

- *A Honda Accord worth $20,000*

- *A home worth $300,000*

- *$7000 in cash*

- *$200,000 in retirement savings in a 401(k)*

- *Total assets: $527,000*

Sam also has the following debts:

- *A car loan of $17,000 on the Honda*
- *A mortgage for $240,000 on his home*
- *$4000 in credit card debts*
- *$30,000 in student loans*
- *Total liabilities: $291,000*

Sam's net worth in this scenario is $236,000.

The financial statement that shows your "net worth" would be the equivalent of a company's "balance sheet." In this case, Sam is worth about a quarter of a million dollars and might be feeling pretty good about himself.

So why is this number so important? Net worth boils down to exactly how many dollars an individual has to their name across all of their financial positions. It's also the number most folks try to increase as much as possible. It gives the individual a clear picture of their financial position across all of their financial accounts and possessions.

Separating Real and False Net Worth

The goal of this book is not to increase one's net worth, as it is commonly calculated, but instead to help the reader attain early financial freedom. Therefore, we must focus on buying and building real assets, not false ones. Commonly calculated net worth includes things like equity in homes, retirement accounts, and cars. These false assets do not generate income and are actually in some cases liabilities to the owner. They soak up dollars that could otherwise be deployed to buy real assets, or to extend one's financial runway. A home, for example, comes with a mortgage payment. Far from expediting early financial freedom, the owner is forced to generate *more* investment income than someone without a large mortgage payment and monthly upkeep expense. The same is true for cars and other luxuries that many people list as assets. Do not focus on increasing net worth as commonly calculated if you desire early financial freedom. Instead, track your real net worth, as comprised of real assets and cash and cash equivalents less debts and obligations. Focus on building wealth that directly works toward your goals, rather than wealth that cannot be harnessed in the near term to produce income or reliable appreciation.

What does one seeking early financial freedom care if they have $200,000 in retirement accounts? If that person is under thirty years old, they may have trouble accessing those funds without penalty for over thirty years! That retirement account is a false asset which doesn't have any direct impact on day-to-day decision-making, or really even long-term decision-making (if ten or more years is considered long-term). Retirement accounts may only be considered part of this equation if they can be accessed far in advance of retirement age, or are a meaningful part of the current financial decision-making process. While it's not bad to have the retirement account, it's not useful to one whose goal is to secure early financial freedom.

If the goal is to become financially free, then we only care about those aspects of net worth that are directly relevant to that goal. Real net worth excludes much of Sam's net worth in the example previously discussed. That said, it's certainly useful to remain up to date on your both your real and false assets. You should keep an eye on the value of your retirement accounts, home equity, car, other items, and resources you own that are of material value, just as you should know the value of your real assets and cash. If you aren't paying constant attention in this game of finance, you will lose. Whether through theft, ticky-tack fees charged by sneaky banks or credit companies, or by making an obvious mistake, those who don't pay close attention to their assets and to where their money is going will slowly lose in the game of money.

The solution? Track both types of net worth—track your commonly calculated net worth and your real net worth. For example, you might track the former with one software tool and the latter with another.

If you don't know your net worth (real or commonly calculated) at the moment and are not regularly checking up on it, then this might be one of those tasks that you set about completing immediately. There's no point in playing the game of finance if you can't even keep score.

Calculating Real Net Worth

We've already demonstrated commonly calculated net worth for Sam. Here's how Sam would calculate his real net worth:

Sam has the following real assets to his name:
- *$7000 in cash*
- *Total usable assets: $7000*

Sam also has the following debts:
- *A car loan of $17,000 on the Honda*

- *A mortgage for $240,000 on his home*
- *$4000 in credit card debts*
- *$30,000 in student loans*
- *Total liabilities: $291,000*

Sam's usable net worth is negative $284,000.

How did this happen? Well, Sam made several key mistakes that far too many middle-class Americans make:

- He bought a financed car.
- He bought a luxury home with a huge mortgage.
- He got himself a financed degree.
- He failed to build any significant wealth outside of a retirement account.

Folks, this is likely what most of America considers a strong financial position, and it's absurd. A lifetime of "smart" decisions and Sam is in a $284,000 financial hole. Another way of expressing this is to say Sam has $284,000 in debts against his ability to make big life decisions that would disrupt his current income or lifestyle. This is why Sam has no choice but to continue to work his job or one very much like it for decades. He is clearly not on a path toward attaining financial freedom anytime soon.

Notice that while false assets are not included in the calculation of real net worth, *debt* associated with those assets is. Purchasing a false asset with debt is double trouble. The asset doesn't assist in the pursuit of early financial freedom, and interest-bearing debt is assumed by the purchaser. Do not purchase false assets with debt if you seek early financial freedom! This is why buying luxuries on credit is such a drag on middle-class America's finances. Financed cars, boats, trucks, TVs, computers, and the like are a double-whammy as they aren't assets that serve the goal of financial freedom, and the debts must be counted against their financial position.

So What Should Sam Do?

Do you understand why parts I and II of this book are so important? Make the effort to move through those sections, and build after-tax cash reserves or their equivalents. Use those dollars to purchase real assets that generate income and are likely to appreciate.

Too many people attempt to move toward early financial freedom from a position like Sam's. Sam is in far worse position than the guy starting from scratch. Sam has to reject choices he's accepted as a smart, normal, and natural progression of adult life, and completely start over in order to begin building assets in a way that will bring about early financial freedom.

If your position is like Sam's and you wish to move toward early financial freedom, you'll have to accept the fact your financial choices to this point in life have resulted in a several hundred thousand dollar hole. You will need to begin to accurately track your finances with a clear understanding of your real net worth, and it might not be pretty. You will need to slowly and steadily begin to climb out of that hole, and accept that you're at the first step of the financial journey and need to begin saving money—after tax—that can be used *today*. Otherwise, you will struggle to do anything other than maintain your current position in life.

Sam needs to get serious about building wealth and immediately make some drastically different choices if he wishes to achieve early financial freedom. Sam isn't going to like any of this advice:

- First, he needs to harness the $60,000 in his home equity by selling his home and purchasing a house hack or far cheaper primary residence.

- Second, he needs to sell his car and buy a used one with $3000 to $7000 cash.

- Third, he needs to design an efficient lifestyle to begin saving thousands of dollars per month.

- Fourth, he needs to start paying down his personal debts (especially the credit card debt) and get them to zero.

- Fifth, he needs to stop contributing to his retirement account and instead focus on building real assets with surplus savings—assets that will help him bring about early financial freedom.

If Sam heeds this advice, he will spend the next several years rapidly building real wealth that gives him real options in life. No longer will he be chained to that mortgage, job, and vesting 401(k) interests. Sam will soon have tens of thousands, and not too much later will have hundreds of thousands of dollars in real, tangible assets like stocks and bonds, investment real estate, and a sizable cash position. In a few short years, he could buy back all of his prior luxuries with cash and have the option to walk away from work entirely.

Of course, this is fantasyland.

Sam isn't going to sell his house and cramp his style. Sam isn't going to sell his car. Sam isn't going to cut back on his spending, so that he all of a sudden starts saving thousands of dollars per month outside of his retirement account. Unfortunately, Sam and people like him typically make excuses, not change. Sam will not give up his house, his fancy SUV, or even start packing lunch.

The best we can hope for is to plant a seed in Sam's mind and to help Sam understand that most of his assets are really liabilities—or at best, are useless, if he wishes to attain early financial freedom. Sam will hopefully keep this in mind over the next few years, and when he gets a raise, won't correspondingly increase his spending but use that extra money toward paying down debts. After a few more years and a few more raises, Sam will have paid off those debts and begin to start investing outside of his retirement account.

We can hope that Sam will slowly begin making changes in his life that move him toward early financial freedom. When Sam's kids start school, he might find opportunities to use after-school programs instead of an expensive babysitter. In ten years, when Sam sells his home, he'll buy a reasonable replacement, instead of the biggest, fanciest one he qualifies for. Slowly but surely, his position will improve, and one day, he will finally have a positive real net worth, and maybe, just maybe, he'll bring some options back into his life.

Sam! I wish I could save you those decades. I wish I could impress upon you the financial consequences of your decisions in those early years, and the abundance that could be yours if you let go of your biggest "assets" and harnessed the wealth you've trapped in them to produce real returns elsewhere.

If only you had avoided those purchases! If only you could have invested in a house hack! If only you could have accumulated some cash so that you could make a big trip, travel the world, or otherwise do the things you really wanted in life! But, in failing to do that, I hope at least, that you begin to build a little wealth outside of your home equity and retirement accounts. I hope you focus your financial strategy around increasing that wealth from now on. And I hope that eventually, slowly but surely, you're able to buy some freedom back into your life. I hope that you buy yourself the power to decide whether and where to work, and what you do during the best part of your day, during the best part of the week, during the best years of your life.

If you resemble Sam, you'll likely need to make a number of changes in many important parts of your life to pursue early financial freedom. And, you will need to honestly calculate your own current position and track the changes over time, with a clear understanding of the consequences of your decisions.

The Second Financial Metric: Spending

Spending should be the metric over which a salaried employee has the most control. Because of this high degree of control, you should pay close attention to your performance when it comes to spending money. There are many ways to track your spending. One thing they all have in common is that for each you must keep a record of each and every transaction you spend money on! There's no getting around this, as you cannot guess at your expenses, you have to see them in black and white for your decision-making to be fully informed.

This can be automatic, or require extreme diligence. It's likely that much of the target audience of this book spends the majority of their money with credit and debit cards, or online. If that's true for you, then the two software products mentioned earlier in the chapter—Mint.com and Personal Capital—will automatically track and bucket these expenses for you. If you don't use one of those software products, you can simply download the transaction history electronically recorded by your bank and credit card company and enter it into a spreadsheet.

In the old days, this used to be much more difficult—folks would have to either keep receipts for every purchase they made and manually log them, or recopy expenses from bank statements they received in the mail. Don't be lost in the last century. In the twenty-first century, we can automatically track and categorize our spending with the help of the awesome software at Mint and Personal Capital. Obviously, you will need to keep track of cash expenses by manually entering them into the software.

Using Mint as an example, a $50 expense for a meal out would be recorded as a "restaurant" expense. However, some expenses will go unrecognized by Mint. You will need to spend the time to categorize and regularly review your expenses. Once per month is fine, and this can be completed in less than ten minutes.

You can bucket your expenses into whatever categories you like, but you should understand at a high level, what you spend on your lifestyle, and what spending is related to your career. As the goal is early financial freedom, spending related to maintaining your career (such as your daily commuting expense) shouldn't be counted toward your lifestyle expense. This spending will be eliminated when you transition out of wage-paying work.

Do You Need a Budget?

The topic of budgeting seems to be immensely popular among financial writers. As we are discussing how and why to track your finances, specifically spending here, the topic of making a budget should be addressed. As briefly touched on in chapter 1, a budget (a detailed outline of what you plan to spend in the next week or month) isn't necessary for those serious about pursuing early financial freedom. If you agree with the basic premise of this book, then it will be clear to you that every time you spend money, you are by definition prioritizing that purchase over the more rapid attainment of financial freedom. Spending decisions are made and avoided in the moment, and every purchase is a penalty that delays your freedom. While there are transactions that are worth delaying financial freedom, the pattern that works for you should become clear very quickly.

If that's your mindset, then there shouldn't be any wasted spending and only those things, which will truly make a difference in the present will have funds directed toward them. If you're so serious about financial freedom that you rarely make purchases frivolously, a budget is unnecessary. If, on the other hand, you find a significant chunk of your spending is on trivial things that a budget might prevent, you are wise to develop one.

Regardless of whether you use a budget, it's still wise to track your spending very carefully, and look for holes in your financial position where money leaks through on a monthly basis. For example, it's possible that you signed up for a subscription a few months ago and forgot about it. Each month, you pay that subscription fee needlessly. The only way to avoid this is to regularly review each expense in the prior month.

The purpose of tracking your spending isn't to guide your day-to-day spending decisions, which will depend on opportunities and the whimsical nature of your day-to-day moods, but to diagnose trends that are significantly impacting your financial position on a regular basis. The point of tracking your spending is so you can use the information to make big life decisions in ways that will truly make a meaningful difference. It is at this point where the decisions become the most personal. You will have to analyze significant transactions, categorize your spending, and then determine where you're spending too much. You can use the information to determine if there are any areas of your life in which you can make a significant change that will positively impact your financial position.

The powerful results that come from consistently analyzing your spending are twofold. First, with consistent analysis, you will spot opportunities to save large amounts of money in your largest expense categories. Obviously, your expenses picture won't be exactly the same as the Average Joe's, outlined in chapter 2. You will need to understand your current spending to conduct effective analysis of your own position and spot the largest areas for improvement.

Second, you will begin to paint a clear picture of the cost of your desired lifestyle, enabling you to plan accordingly and decide how much passive income is necessary for you to generate to retire early. What you will learn from this consistent analysis may amaze you. Many people believe that life gets more and more expensive with age. One that tracks their financial position and intelligently cuts out the waste will find the opposite to be true. You'll find with routine analysis and in taking consistently intelligent action toward reducing your expenses that your lifestyle costs less and less with each year, instead of more and more. The closer to financial freedom you get, the less you'll spend, the more fun you'll have, and the less you'll need to work!

The Third Financial Metric: Income

Tracking income is kind of pointless for an Average Joe earning a full-time salary with little opportunity to increase his earnings. Clearly, he is aware of his salary and the amount of money he is paid with his paycheck.

If that's true for you, then you can come back to this section in a few months or perhaps a year or two, when you have taken some action, invested $10,000 or more, gotten a new job with performance-based pay, and/or started a side hustle. On the other hand, if you have a few investments, have streams of income outside of the standard W2 paycheck, and have some control over that income, then you can and should be keeping meticulous records on that income, and regularly checking in on trends and looking for opportunities to improve.

Be sure to track that income which is directly relevant to your goal: Passive income that can be used to satisfy the financial freedom equation. Passive income, depending on how you invest, may or may not be under your direct control or within your ability to influence. If it's within your control, you will want to take actions to remove the risks of losing it and to increase it. If it's not within your control (like dividend income from index fund investing, for example), then you simply want to measure it and watch it grow, so that you can systematically track your progress toward financial freedom and calculate the point at which you are comfortable with leaving wage-paying work.

Here's an example: Adam works a sales job that's part commission, part salary; he also invests in real estate and stocks. Here are the ways he makes money, after taxes, each month:

Salary: $2000

Commissions: $1500

Real estate rental income: $500

Real estate appreciation: $1000

Real estate principal reduction: $500

Stock appreciation: $1000

Stock Dividends: $250

In this case, Adam is building wealth at a rate of about $6750 per month or $81,000 per year, in spite of the fact that he only earns $42,000 per year at his job. That's excellent, and higher than the average American, but it's a point you can reach in just a few years by following the process outlined in this book. Adam has appropriately broken out his wealth increases into the following categories and receives the following insight from this analysis:

- First, his passive income is $750 per month ($500 from his rental property and $250 from stock dividends)—Adam will have to decide if that kind of passive income is likely to be sustained or if this was a particularly good or poor month for passive income generation.

- Second, Adam's stock appreciation and his real estate equity are both outside of his control, as he did nothing to improve the property. While these gains are nice, they are not something he should spend much time worrying about.

- Third, Adam's salary is unlikely to change significantly, but his commissions are quite interesting. They make up a large fraction of his income. Adam should spend quite a bit of time diving into his commissions and learn which types of sales produce the most income, and which prospects are most likely to buy.

In this income analysis, the commissions are the real prize. They are the real prize, because they are the only type of income over which Adam has direct control, and they're significant, given his overall income. He can directly impact the amount of money he earns by increasing his sales output.

The Fourth Financial Metric: Time

Most people have no idea how they spend their time. They don't know what they do in the morning, they don't know what they do at work, and they don't know what they do on the weekend. Most people have no idea if their actions tend toward their goals (in fact, most people don't have goals).

Early financial freedom is your goal. Write it down. Run the calculations. Determine what is realistic in the next year, the next quarter, the next week, and today. Take action that moves you toward that goal *every day*. You don't have to just do this with early financial freedom; you should be doing it with the other big goals in your life!

Every day, determine what you are going to do to attain early financial freedom. It doesn't have to be a big thing—it can be something small like, "set up Mint" or "spend ten minutes looking for cheaper apartment options on Craigslist." Write down your small goal in your daily log, and cross it off when it's completed.

Every week, determine what you are going to do to attain early financial freedom. This goal will be slightly bigger than the daily goal or a set of small daily goals that you will complete each day. For example, "Discover My Real Net Worth, Commonly Calculated Net Worth, Income, and Monthly Expenses."

Every quarter, determine what you are going to do to attain early financial freedom. Your quarterly goals will be large objectives that might take others an entire year to complete. You will accomplish them in months or weeks because you track your time and take daily actions to hasten the achievement of your goals.

Every year, determine what you are going to do to attain early financial freedom. You should be able to go from a standing start with few assets to well over $100,000 in real net worth within three to five years. Your annual goals should be set up to accelerate through the stages of wealth creation outlined in parts I, II, and III. There is no reason you, as a median wage earner, cannot surpass the $100,000 mark in three years if you follow the advice in this book and act intelligently in pursuit of your goals. The time between accruing the first $100,000 to full financial freedom varies dramatically, and is dependent on the opportunities that one exploits, the investments they make, and their lifestyle expenses.

This approach to tracking time, and setting and achieving goals, isn't some intricate success log from a success guru. It's not a proven success "formula" or "secret." It's just a plain set of documents produced in Microsoft Word. Print them off every day, week, month, quarter, and year, and try to complete them every day. Decide what you want, put it on paper, and work toward your goals!

Sample daily, weekly, monthly, quarterly, and annual logs are provided in the Appendix. Do you have to use this structure? You are certainly welcome to it, and can create a copy of a template at any time. That said, everyone operates differently, has different priorities, and has different goals. It's far better if you just view those templates and build your own. List out your top priorities (no more than two or three!) for each day/week/quarter/year in any manner you choose. Then, figure out the tasks, habits, or relationships that you believe will be most impactful in advancing those interests.

However, one thing you must do is use some sort of system to track your time. Regardless of how you go about setting goals and tracking your progress, you must intentionally complete the task that you believe is the highest priority and most likely to move you toward your goal each day. Occasionally, you will be unable to complete the task that you assigned yourself. Make sure those days are rare, and that you complete at least one easy thing that does move you forward.

Tailor your daily log and how you allocate time in the day to the pursuit of opportunities that are relevant. Someone writing a book will have a meticulous plan with careful time blocking, while a salesman will prospect with any free time, but spend as much time as possible on quality leads.

Optimal daily planning and tracking comes down to being very intentional about the most important things in your day, and setting aside several hours of dedicated quiet time toward the completion of that task. However, you also cannot systematize your interaction with truly important people in your day, and will need to set aside not *time* blocks, but *action blocks* with regards to reaching out and meeting with other people and helping them.

Make sure you are prioritizing the people who are important to you, and that they have a primary place of importance in your day. If you are not naturally an outgoing person, make sure you include important people in your daily log and do something small to show your appreciation for them. This can come in the form of a quick thank you note to a client, reaching out to someone who you connected with a few months ago to see how they are progressing with a certain issue, or messaging an old friend you've lost contact with over the years.

How to Track Your Time

Your daily log, however formatted, should allow you to track your time. One viable method for doing this is to categorize your day into time blocks like the following:

- ✔ Early morning (before 9:00 a.m.)
- ✔ Late morning (9:00 a.m. to 12:00 p.m.)
- ✔ Early afternoon (12:00 p.m. to 2:30 p.m.)
- ✔ Late afternoon (2:30 p.m. to 5:00 p.m.)
- ✔ Early evening (5:00 p.m. to 7:30 p.m.)
- ✔ Late evening (after 7:30 p.m.)

Simply set an alarm throughout the day and write a brief summary of what you did in each time block. No, you don't have to be productive the entire time, and obviously, don't do this in a way that distracts those around you. You'll be amazed at what this simple habit can do for you in terms of getting you to focus in on what's really important. But be brutally honest. If you are honest, you'll see things like "I can't remember a single important thing I did in this time period" or "I wasted this time doing such and such" or "Didn't feel great, watched football" on your list.

Failure is fine. Nobody's perfect, and you should not try to be. But, if you can get to the point where most of those time blocks in your day include at least one action that moves you toward your goals, you will make incredible progress. You have six chances each day to take at least one important action toward your goals.

How to Analyze Your Findings

In the language of businesses, the bit that we just covered—on keeping track of our net worth, spending, income, and time—is called accounting. Few people like to do this type of work, yet it's by keeping consistent records that you can then go back, analyze your data, and make decisions that will lead to improvements. Some people don't like to do this, find it tedious, and aren't interested in tracking and analyzing their financial picture.

If you don't enjoy this work, but wish to rapidly attain early financial freedom, then I have this to say to you: *Too bad*. Do it anyway. Nobody likes doing this, but it's what wealthy people do. It's like working out. If you want to be fit, you have to exercise. If you want to be rich, you need to have an up-to-date understanding of your financial picture, and need to consistently review your position and progress. It is the ability to analyze, to look at, and study your past patterns of spending, that allows you to access the information needed to make real changes to your behavior that will lead to financial progress.

While accounting is important for its own sake, in the context of this book, the value that it provides is really in its ability to allow you to make decisions. If you already have a good grasp on your finances, or spend, save, and earn like a typical American, then much of the analysis provided in chapter 2 on the spending side will apply and prove a powerful tool in assisting your ability to build wealth. Cutting out your huge rent/mortgage payments, your car payment, and the debilitating portion of your food and dining budget are likely to be the key bits of analysis that the majority of Americans need to hear. If you're typical, then the data from your personal financial picture will only tell you the story of Average Joe, and the actions suggested in chapters 1 and 2 apply directly to you.

However, if you wish to pursue financial freedom beyond what can be covered in just one book speaking to a national audience, you'll need to compile your own analysis and understand your own behavior. Track your expenses and time and use the information that you compile to help you make decisions where it counts most!

Materiality

Back in chapter 9, we demonstrated just how silly it is to sell water bottles outside the stadium in order to earn an "investment" return. Materiality also applies here, in the analysis of spending, income, and investment performance. Those trying to make decisions and get use out of tracking and analyzing their financial picture need to group expenses together and focus their effort on decisions of significant importance.

If the decision will impact less than 1 to 2 percent of your monthly expenditures, it's probably not material. Make a decision that appears reasonable and spend your time on bigger issues. This doesn't mean ignore them.

The cable bill might comprise $500 per year, or 1 percent of your after-tax income—and that's an expense you should cut. But, if you wish to pursue early financial freedom, that decision should be obvious. You shouldn't fret over that decision for hours and hours, building complicated projections. You should eliminate that expense entirely, as soon as possible.

Furthermore, don't make personal sacrifices over small amounts of money. If it saves $5 to shop at a supermarket that's thirty minutes away, and you have a grocery store next door, save yourself the hour and buy groceries next door. The difference between the two decisions is immaterial and you needlessly inconvenience yourself for a trivial amount of money. Similarly, trying to clip coupons to save a few bucks on a trip to the supermarket is silly. Buying pots, pans, Tupperware, and trying out a few recipes that will help you consistently make and enjoy your own breakfasts, lunches, and dinners regularly will save you hundreds, if not thousands, of dollars per year. That's a pursuit you should put some time, energy, and analysis into.

Understand what's impactful. It is ridiculous *not* to spend large amounts of time assessing the various consequences of decisions regarding major parts of your financial picture. Yet it's equally ridiculous to spend tons of time on the trivial parts.

Vacations are a favorite example. Many people spend more time planning their vacations than planning their financial future. Average Joe spends less than $2000 per year on vacation. This is less than 5 percent of his income, so it's not something he should be obsessing over. Yes, he should attempt to get a great deal with a few hours of work. But, far more time over the course of his year should be spent on planning where he's going to live, how he's going to transport himself, and what he's going to eat.

The point of this example is to show you that what you need to look at with a watchful eye and what you need to become an expert at, are the things that matter significantly in your budget. For almost everyone, that includes food, housing, and transportation. You have no excuse for failing to educate yourself about the true costs of those three categories and not to seriously explore all possibilities for making big improvements there. It is up to you to track and analyze your financial picture regularly to see what other areas of spending and life merit your attention.

Conclusion

Financial modeling, data analysis, accounting, forecasting—so much of the business world is built upon these concepts. Nowadays we have infinitely more ability to accumulate and analyze data, and businesses are taking advantage of it. You as an individual need to be doing the same if you want to gain control of your income and pursue early financial freedom. But, equally important are the intangibles. The human factor. The ability to challenge the unchallengeable.

Yes, tracking the numbers that correlate to the goals you want to achieve, and the resulting data analysis of that tracking is critical to your long-term success. You must be able to recognize and continually improve upon the financial levers in your life. But, never forget that data can only tell so much. When your gut, your instinct, your *feelings* tell you that something surely ought to work over what the data is telling you, think twice before acting. The real key to being effective is to find solutions that make sense logically, emotionally, *and* are backed up by data. If you *know* a client isn't likely to be successful with what you are selling them, don't sell it to them! If you *feel* there's something wrong with that high paying job you've been offered, don't take it! The data is *half* of the story. No more, no less. It is completely acceptable to gather all of the data, acknowledge the story being told by the data, then *totally dismiss it,* and make a decision that's not supported by the data. Don't make a decision without having the data. Know your numbers, but don't be afraid to do something that you feel is right, just because the data seems to indicate something else.

If you look at things logically, and ask the obvious questions that no one else is asking, you can make incredible strides toward your goals, financial and otherwise. Do not overestimate the benefits of statistical analysis on its own, but don't make decisions in ignorance of the numbers either. Numbers tell a story, and they don't lie. $10,000 spent per year on "auto and transport" is telling you a story. It's up to you to decide if that was worthwhile (you met with hundreds of clients all over the state or drove across the country on a life changing yearlong trip!) or wasted (you lived ten miles farther away from work than you needed to in an average suburban neighborhood, instead of in a near perfect replica of your neighborhood that exists less than five miles from work).

Chapter 13
Habits and Their Impact on Financial Freedom

Many people understand what they need to do to become wealthy. It's straightforward: save; earn; aggressively invest the difference. Repeat and scale until early financial freedom is achieved. All it takes is consistency, intelligent effort, and time. However, progress can be drastically slowed and financially freedom needlessly delayed due to small mistakes and bad habits that compound over time.

Too often, folks complain they don't have the time to start moving toward financial freedom. While it might not be feasible to earn a large side income in just a few hours per night (which is why you need to change jobs and focus on something with a workday that has the potential to scale), you *do* have plenty of time in the day to make significant progress toward financial freedom. And it's likely that you are wasting a significant portion of that time. Enough such that you could redirect wasted activity that provides little happiness or joy toward pursuits that are in line with your goals. Never before in human history has man had more access to opportunity. There are an unlimited number of productive ways toward which you can direct your intelligence, passion, and attentiveness—but an equally unlimited number of distractions pulling you away from those things that *actually matter*.

Most people struggle to produce and work toward meaningful goals in light of the vast number of distractions that confront us in everyday life. This chapter won't be pretty. It will point out the bad habits that you know to be true, the ones that are holding you back from success. It will force you to decide if the attainment of early financial freedom is worth the change that you will have to make in your everyday activities.

This isn't to say that these habits need to be eliminated entirely from your life. It is to say that they need to be significantly reduced and not a primary component of your day-to-day life, if you are looking to become successful at an early age. The problem isn't in indulging in these behaviors from time to time and when in certain moods. The problem is when these activities become *habits, every day*, as part of your routine.

You're not going to like this. But, you need to hear it.

Cut These Ten Habits Out of Your Life

Habit #1: TV/Netflix

Netflix and 99.9 percent of television programming have absolutely nothing to offer in terms of steering you toward the things you really want in life. They are a distraction, a waste of time, and worst of all, an opportunity cost. You could be doing something better with almost every second. This is especially true in *selecting* a TV show or movie to watch, or in combination with the inability to instantly make trivial decisions.

If you care about your goals, television and video programming will no longer be a part of your day-to-day life. Average Joe spends 2.8 hours of his day watching TV, including weekends. That's two hours forty-eight minutes *per day*. Think about the life you could have if you just redirected half of that toward your goals, and the other half toward hanging out with close friends and family! TV has no place in the day-to-day life of the ambitious early retiree.

Habit #2: Sports Entertainment

Professional, college, and amateur sports are a distraction. You could be doing something better with that time in almost every situation. This isn't to say that you should cut sports out of your life entirely, but it does mean that being a rabid fan of the local NFL team or watching every game in the NCAA basketball tournament is costing you. Big time. It's understandable to watch big games, and even to follow a club, but understand the opportunity cost of becoming a rabid sports fan. Those who make their favorite sports team a massive part of their day and identity become . . . great sports fans.

Is that really who you want to be?

Sports entertainment has no place in the day-to-day life of the ambitious early retiree.

Habit #3: A Luxury Residence Far from Work

We covered housing decisions in chapter 4, but it needs to be stated that in addition to the house itself costing a fortune, luxury living is in itself a *bad habit* that's expensive and time consuming to maintain. With the luxury home comes luxury furniture, and with the luxury furniture comes fancy decorations, and with the fancy decorations come the inevitable deluge of expensive crap needed to match and go along with them. It takes time, energy, and money to set up and maintain a luxury residence and all the trappings that go along with that lifestyle. It promotes other financial decisions that detract from financial freedom.

This kind of living bleeds folks dry in the form of rent/mortgage payments that preclude them from building wealth, forces them to spend large amounts of unproductive time commuting to and from work, and incentivizes them to stay at home—often alone, bored, or at best, tired from a long day or week working and commuting. Luxury living is often expensive to maintain and furnish, and encourages other behaviors (such as TV, sports, eating out, nightlife, and shopping) that further detract from goals. Many folks who choose such living situations also purchase an expensive automobile to compensate for their long commute and match the high standard of living embodied by their personal home. Rarely do you encounter the lady, with the immaculate and expensive home, dressed in the latest clothes from fancy stores, driving a Civic.

Many folks who feel stuck and frustrated with their lives compound that frustration daily on the way to and from work in their luxury car (which is stuck in traffic because of their poor choice in the location of their residence relative to traffic cycles, in addition to being far from work). They are also forced to allocate time toward maintaining their home, which they fail to see is a distraction to their higher objectives, misguidedly believing that their home is an "asset" to their social status or in the case of suburban homeowners, a "wealth-building" investment.

"Sacrificing" your luxury residence (at least in the short-term) for a downgrade closer to work might just be the single most powerful thing you can do in the pursuit of your dreams, both in freeing up your time and your money.

Luxury living has no place in the day-to-day life of the ambitious early retiree.

Habit #4: Eating Out

There are occasions when meeting someone for lunch makes sense. Catching up with a friend, family member, potential business associate, or coworker over lunch or a beer can be a great use of time. Using reasonable restaurants this way isn't a bad thing. If you meet potential connections, mentors, or other people who are likely to help you move toward your goals, then do that regularly, every single day, if you can.

On the other hand, if going out to lunch, dinner, or worse, breakfast by yourself or with the same small group is your go-to move, then it's likely eating your dreams. Bring a lunch instead. Cut your eating time and find something productive to do on your lunch break instead.

Eating out regularly has the following drawbacks:

- It's *expensive.*

- It's *time-consuming.*

- It's *unhealthy.*

Eating out is acceptable when you are invited to an event or when it's the best way to meet critical people—people who can help you get to where you want to be or people who you love. If you are meeting clients, contacts, and potential mentors, keep it up. Far too often, however, we fool ourselves into thinking that a lunch was "productive," when it was really a net loss to our wallets, productivity, and health. Don't fall into that trap. Make your own food, and default to a healthy, efficient, delicious, and self-prepared meal.

Eating out routinely has no place in the day-to-day life of the ambitious early retiree.

Habit #5: Social Media

Facebook, LinkedIn, Twitter, Instagram, Pinterest, and other major social media channels are now part of everyday business vernacular. It's actually perfectly acceptable, even mandatory in some cases, for folks to be on these networks as a normal part of their job. And these tools do provide value—they help us to reach more people, share our content, achievements, and milestones with others, and generate business. The problem with these apps is that they are designed to distract you. They are designed to keep your attention for as long as possible and to suck you back in as frequently as possible. That's their job. That's how they make money—huge money. And they are very, very good at it.

If you are serious about success and achieving some big goals, then social media isn't something you spend all day on. Social media is something you use efficiently, effectively, and succinctly to share, access, and collaborate on those issues that are relevant to your goals. If you want to see how your friends are doing and keep up with their lives, check in once a week with the feeds of just those you care about. Aimlessly trolling social media has no place in the day-to-day life of the ambitious early retiree.

Habit #6: Music at Work

Ah, I can hear the shouts of disapproval already. Music in and of itself is a wonderful thing and is a wonderful way to entertain yourself. If you need a few minutes of your favorite song in the morning or like classical music while you work or need a few amped-up songs to get pumped for your workout, obviously it would be a mistake to cut that out.

But music is not helping you achieve your goals when you are listening to your favorite rap, country, rock, pop, or typical popular music at work. That country station on the way to work can and should be swapped out for a book on tape or podcast on real estate, business, personal development, or something similarly productive. Music distracts you when you are working toward your goals. Period. This has been scientifically proven with the possible exception of listening to music within a narrow band of acceptable listening. Stop listening when you are trying to be productive, creative, or are otherwise involved in making important life or business decisions.

Furthermore, even when you are *not* working directly toward your goals, free time and mindless, repetitive chores can be far more productive when you listen to content that helps you grow in business, personal life, or develop new skills. If you are listening to your favorite music artist, you must acknowledge that you are at that point prioritizing the recreational pursuit of listening to that song over your career, personal development, or other life goals. You could be doing better.

Music doesn't directly take away from your ability to do other things, but it *could* be replaced with something that will actually help move you toward your goals, and it's a distraction. Over a long time period, such as a year, the person who forgoes music for self-education and development audio will have a massive advantage over the music listener.

Typically popular music has no place in the day-to-day life of the ambitious early retiree. And, it's probably a good idea to swap out listening to the same song for the thirtieth time with an audiobook or podcast that can help you advance your career every now and then.

Habit #7: Nightlife

Occasionally, you will meet someone so deluded that they argue that getting drunk and stumbling around bars is productive. To quote a particularly hilarious absurdity: "Two hundred dollars a month [in savings] isn't going to make the dent that a $60,000 pay raise will after spending all those nights out networking."[1]

If you believe in this approach, you are full of it. Don't kid yourself that getting drunk and going out to clubs and bars past midnight is in any way productive to your higher goals. Those nights are fun, plain and simple. But the people who you meet out on the town, at the bar, are *not* likely to help you proceed toward your goals and are not interested in advancing those causes when you meet them. Like the rest of these habits, indulging occasionally isn't going to devastate your progress, but it's going to slow you down. Recognize that, and temper yourself appropriately.

Nightlife has no place in the day-to-day life of the ambitious early retiree.

Habit #8: Shopping

There are some items in your life that can make a serious difference in your productivity, and there are some items that will last much longer than others. For example, it's quite reasonable to spend a large amount of time selecting a new mattress, investment property, computer, or insurance policy, as that might significantly improve the quality of your life, your ability to produce effectively on a day to day basis, your peace of mind, and your financial position.

However, do not spend a large amount of time comparing options between things that are extraordinarily similar. This is a disturbing habit that combines a seeming lack of purpose with a needless waste of money. Know what you need, get in, get out, and then do something that works toward your goals or that you truly enjoy! Like many of the other habits on this list, shopping aimlessly is a waste of time and money, especially when shopping for items that are so obviously not of benefit for more than a brief

---

[1] Martin, *If You Have Savings In Your 20s, You're Doing Something Wrong*, Online.

snapshot in time.

Shopping should only take as long as it takes to understand what you need and the tradeoffs between price and quality. Decisions only need to be brooded over when the stakes are high.

Shopping as a hobby has no place in the day-to-day life of the ambitious early retiree.

Habit #9: The Snooze Button

The snooze button is the ambitious person's greatest ally. It keeps the competition in bed, where they can't compete! Better yet, it makes them groggy, unproductive, and way worse off than if they had just gotten out of bed in the first place.

When that snooze button goes off and you have to awaken to hit it, that's it. It's over. You aren't going to get any more productive rest, you aren't going to be better off in fifteen minutes, thirty minutes, or an hour while your alarm keeps going off every ten minutes. In fact, you are actually making yourself way worse off than if you just got out of bed the first time the alarm goes off—at least from the standpoint of benefitting from sleep.[2]

The snooze button costs more than the few extra minutes of time you unproductively spend in bed. It's costing you the next several hours of productivity, mental sharpness, and production.

Waking up is a mindset. When that alarm goes off, get up quickly and be grateful for whatever sleep you got. Snoozing for more won't help.

The snooze button has no place in the day-to-day life of the ambitious early retiree.

Habit #10: The "I Want to Try to Do Everything" Mentality

Millennials, for their part, have been widely documented as valuing experiences over other types of consumption. There's nothing wrong with this mindset, and indeed, one of the benefits of early financial freedom comes in the ability to have significantly more unique experiences than peers that work forty hours per week with three weeks vacation. However, taken to the extreme, this mindset results in the following outcome: *They have a ton of shallow experiences in a large number of areas, thus becoming fairly lousy at a lot of different things. This comes at the expense of becoming excellent in just a*

---

[2] If you want to know more, check out CNN's, "Is the Snooze Button Bad for You?" By Erinn Bucklan - http://www.cnn.com/2014/02/06/health/upwave-snooze-button/.

few areas that they truly enjoy.

If the desire to experience new cities, lifestyles, and experiences is too strong, then it holds you back from self-development and mastery of any of the cultures, hobbies, or passions that you seek to truly experience. You can't commit to any projects or visions that will help you make an impact on the world or that lead to success if you are too preoccupied with experiencing *everything* the world has to offer. Too many people seem to prioritize having a wide breadth of life experiences, but fail to prioritize having a deep level of expertise or passion about hobbies in a more narrow range.

This isn't to say you shouldn't have hobbies, passions, or pursuits you genuinely love. It's to say that instead of trying to do everything, pick a few things you truly love and develop an intimate level of expertise and knowledge in those areas, instead of trying to overextend into too many new areas of life. You may find you enjoy them far more, and that your recreational pursuits, as a whole, cost less.

By all means, develop new interests outside your comfort zone. Just don't forget that the bulk of your focus should be on your core strengths and those weaknesses that you need to overcome to achieve what you *truly* want.

Being a "jack of all trades, yet a master of none" has no place in the day-to-day life of the ambitious early retiree.

Conclusion

The activities listed above do little to impact day-to-day happiness, and in most cases, when habitually part of day-to-day life, take away from one's ability to lead more meaningful lives. It's possible to lose the forest for the trees and argue that there actually *are* some merits to each of these habits. But, be honest with yourself and cut out the waste. If you can free up just a few hours each day by eliminating bad habits like these, you will discover countless opportunities to pursue your goals. You'll also have more time to spend on pleasures and people who make you truly happy.

Replace the time eaten up by these habits with time spent doing things you truly love and things that will move you toward your goals. You aren't sacrificing anything by giving up this list! You are *giving* yourself a better life! Replace these habits with time spent working out, learning to make and enjoy healthy and delicious meals, hanging out with close friends and family, working on your goals, developing quality new connections, volunteering, and finding mentors.

Chapter 14
Conclusion

Get rich. Stop working for money. Set yourself up for life. And do it as early in life as you possibly can!

You *can* achieve early financial freedom and free yourself from the constraints of wage-paying work. By developing your financial runway, you will be free to pursue your hobbies and passions, and you will be free to start businesses or organizations that can change the world. You will be free to travel the world, living like a local, and experience new cultures in ways that employed professionals could never imagine. You will be free to spend your Tuesday morning at the gym, your Wednesday afternoon at the park, and your Thursday night at a rock concert, with no fear of falling behind at the office. You will be free to raise your children with the best part of your day, during the formative years of your children's lives.

Those who are financially free retain their ability to work for wages and live the lifestyle of their peers, if they choose. The difference is that they, financially, just *don't have to work*. The financially free design their day based on what they *want* to do, not what they *have* to do. They do not allow pitiful excuses, like the fact that they currently "love their job" prevent them from pursuing and maintaining financial freedom. They understand that even if their job and coworkers are incredible today, that things can change tomorrow.

The hardest part of the journey is going from a standing start (little to no net worth) to approximately $100,000. It takes sacrifice to accumulate the first $25,000, hustle to scale that income, and intelligence, knowledge, and creativity to turn accumulated capital into income producing investments that increase in value. Progress seems painfully slow at first, but once you get the ball rolling, it will never stop. Assets continue to grow and snowball, and more and more income is generated with less and less effort.

The first step on the journey toward early financial freedom is the development of a strong positive monthly cash flow and the creation of around one year of financial runway. Those seeking early financial freedom should begin saving as much as they possibly can *today*. You should cut your spending to $1500 to $2000 per month, or lower if possible. You need to build up a reserve of $25,000 through the means described in part I. Then use that money to take a chance on a carefully researched job opportunity, business, or investment that's capable of producing life changing results far more rapidly than your current career track. You should work as hard as possible to continually isolate yourself from the risks and changes in an industry or company, and move away from financial dependence on an employer. Focus on making financial progress such that you could survive for a year without employment. Then five years. Then forever.

It doesn't matter how early financial freedom is achieved, and the process in this book isn't a one-size-fits-all approach. But, for almost every reader not in New York, San Francisco, or Los Angeles, there is one decision that's particularly relevant to this goal: housing. Virtually every other part of the country offers median earners the ability to buy property. There will be no other major financial decision that can make as much impact as buying an investment property as an owner occupant. Move in, and rent out the extra bedrooms or units. Let tenants cover your housing expenses. Live for free. This decision allows you to live rent and mortgage free, to pay down a mortgage using other people's money, and to benefit from appreciation. Those who fail to pursue this incredibly powerful strategy are forced to try to build wealth through less efficient means and will pay the price with years of additional dependence on wage-paying work.

The best-case scenario in many career paths is a 10 percent annual raise, and a promotion every eighteen to twenty-four months. The best-case scenario on that trajectory is that the corporate lackey will be going nowhere fast next year, the year after, and in five years. Don't follow that path. Get out. Find an opportunity that offers the possibility of scaling your income. Understand that the cost of opportunity is frequently a reduction in base salary. Those pursuing early financial freedom put themselves in a position where base salary is irrelevant and where they are able to save substantial amounts of money, even on a modest salary. Put yourself in positions where you can pursue synergistic side hustles and outside income streams. Free yourself to pursue scale and hasten financial freedom, and do not allow your lifestyle costs to creep up when you do experience great success. Instead, work diligently and consistently until your assets are generating passive income in excess of your lifestyle costs. *Work hard. Spend as little as possible.*

Invest the difference aggressively.

Cash is king. While it's not necessary to let large amounts of cash sit around in a bank account at low interest rates, it's wise to ensure it's easily accessible. One way to do this is to keep a large amount of money—perhaps twice the amount that might make sense for a reasonable emergency fund—invested in index funds that can be sold any business day. However accomplished, access to cash is critical, as it will help you handle emergencies with ease, take risks that others could only dream of, and take advantage of investment opportunities unavailable to peers without access to cash.

Track progress. Track expenses. Track income. Track net worth—both "real" and "false" assets. Track *time.* Understand resource allocation, and ruthlessly eliminate inefficiencies, particularly when it comes to low impact tasks. What gets measured gets managed. No one pursuing early financial freedom is above this. Everyone needs to track their spending, and everyone has the ability to take advantage of easy wins or cut out needless mistakes. Make sure you too are taking control and managing your finances, not letting them manage you.

Lastly, eliminate distractions and wasted time, and associate with people and organizations that are synergistic with the goal of financial freedom. Learn from everyone—the wealthy, the poor, and the middle class. Make time for early financial freedom and read relentlessly. The pursuit of early financial freedom doesn't have to consume your leisure time, but it should be woven into your life—where you live, where you work, how you transport yourself, and yes, what you discuss with friends, family, and coworkers. Early financial freedom is a way of life, just as much as it's the satisfaction of a financial equation and it's within your grasp.

Young people are told they can be whatever they want when they grow up. Sadly, dreams do not come true for millions of Americans. They buy themselves into car payments, mortgage payments, timeshares, cable TV subscriptions, and happy hour addictions. They splurge on unhealthy food at restaurants. They work pointless, boring jobs that will soon be automated by machinery and offer little opportunity for scale. But you won't be one of those people. You now have the tools, knowledge, and motivation to become financially free and live your dreams. I'm here to tell you that while you can no longer necessarily be anything you choose, the silver lining is that there is nothing you can't do *with your own money and your own time.* Build your own wealth, buy back your time, and spend both wisely. *Set yourself up for life and live.*

Notes

Brickman, Philip; Dan Coates; Ronnie Janoff-Bulman. *Lottery winners and accident victims: Is happiness relative?* Journal of Personality and Social Psychology, Vol 36(8), Aug 1978, 917–927. http://dx.doi.org/10.1037/0022-3514.36.8.917.

Clark, Patrick. *Debt Is Piling Up Faster for Most Graduate Students—but Not MBAs.* Bloomberg, March 25, 2014. https://www.bloomberg.com/news/articles/2014-03-25/student-loan-debt-piles-up-for-graduate-students-but-not-mbas.

Cost of Owning and Operating Vehicle in U.S. Increases Nearly Two Percent According to AAA's 2013 'Your Driving Costs' Study. AAA Newsroom, April 16, 2013. http://newsroom.aaa.com/2013/04/cost-of-owning-and-operating-vehicle-in-u-s-increases-nearly-two-percent-according-to-aaas-2013-your-driving-costs-study-archive/.

Damodaran, Aswath. *Damdoran Online.* http://pages.stern.nyu.edu/~adamodar/.

Financing Your Wheels: How Much Should I Budget for a Down Payment on a Car? Quicken. https://www.quicken.com/financing-your-wheels-how-much-should-i-budget-down-payment-car

Healery, James. *Average new car price zips 2.6% to $33,560.* USA Today, May 4, 2015. http://www.usatoday.com/story/money/cars/2015/05/04/new-car-transaction-price-3-kbb-kelley-blue-book/ 26690191/

Kylstra, Carolyn. *10 Things Your Commute Does to Your Body.* Time, February 26, 2014. Time.com/9912/10-things-your-commute-does-to-your-body/

Langer, Gary. *Poll: Traffic in the United States.* ABC News, February 13, 2015. http://abcnews.go.com/Technology/Traffic/story?id=485098&page=1.

Martin, Lauren. *If You Have Savings In Your 20s, You're Doing Something Wrong.* EliteDaily, September 16, 2015. http://elitedaily.com/life/savings-20s-something-wrong/1214445/.

Merriman, Paul A. *The genius of Warren Buffett in 23 quotes.* MarketWatch, August 19, 2015. http://www.marketwatch.com/story/the-genius-of-warren-buffett-in-23-quotes-2015-08-19.

Sommeiller, Estelle; Mark Price; Ellis Wazeter. *Income inequality in the U.S. by state, metropolitan area, and county.* Economic Policy Institute, June 16, 2016. http://www.epi.org/publication/income-inequality-in-the-us/.

Appendix
Retirement Accounts

This book considers retirement accounts to be false assets. And, for most Americans, they are. Most Americans do not *intend* to access the money in retirement accounts at an early age. If, however, you *are* willing to develop a plan to harness the money in retirement accounts well in advance of the normal retirement age, there is a way to do so. If you intend to use the money in retirement accounts in advance of retirement age, and to fund early financial freedom, then retirement accounts *can be real assets* for you. Retirement accounts can actually be smart ways to build tax-advantaged wealth for folks who are willing to use them to help plan for early financial freedom. They do *not* count as real net worth if you fail to take advantage of them as part of your plan to attain early financial freedom, or do not intend to. That is why they are not real net worth for the majority of Americans.

Are you ready to turn your retirement accounts into real assets? If so, read on.

The Pre-tax or Tax-deferred Retirement Account

Common pre-tax or "tax-deferred" retirement accounts enable you to avoid paying present taxes on your contributions and instead pay them at a later date.

> *Dave and Virginia are married and earn a combined $200,000 per year. This income is taxed at a marginal tax rate of 28 percent. Combined, they contribute $18,000 to their retirement 401(k). Because this is pre-tax, they are taxed this year on $18,000 less in income. At their 28 percent tax bracket, this means that they save $5040 in taxes this year.*
>
> *Dave and Virginia retire thirty years later. At that point, they*

begin withdrawing from their 401(k) and spend about $75,000 per year. This income might be taxed at around 18 percent. When they withdraw that same $18,000 they contributed thirty years earlier, this means they pay taxes of only $3240, saving them $1800 in taxes overall.

Dave and Virginia earn a very high income that's taxed heavily during the years that they contribute to their 401(k). The 401(k) is an effective way to shield their currently high income from taxes. However, also note that Dave and Virginia expect to receive less income or lower taxed income after they stop working. If that happens, then they will be able to avoid paying taxes on their highly taxed high incomes today, and instead pay fewer taxes when they withdraw that money in the future.

The After-tax Retirement Account

Typically, folks invest for retirement through a Roth IRA to contribute to retirement after-tax. This means that you simply contribute money that would otherwise be available to you, after federal and state taxes have been taken out of your paycheck, and put it into a Roth IRA. Then, when you retire, you are able to withdraw both your contribution *and any gains* on invested funds, tax free, in the future.

Sally and Ian earn $75,000 per year today combined, and are taxed at a rate of 15 percent on their earned income. Each year, they max out their Roth IRAs by contributing $5500 apiece. This money is contributed after-tax, and they forgo other investments and using the money for fun/leisure activities. They invest this money in index funds and earn 10 percent over the next thirty years, entering retirement with a balance of $950,000.

Sally and Ian were also savvy outside of their Roth IRAs and built a substantial real estate empire worth millions of additional dollars by employing the concepts in this book. Thirty years from now, their portfolio will generate almost $300,000 per year in business income and they will enjoy spending close to that amount, as a reward for their decades of intelligent wealth building. As this will place them in a 33 percent tax bracket, they are sure glad that they don't have to pay tax on their Roth IRA withdrawals too!

Sally and Ian are relatively modest earners compared to Dave and Virginia. However, they are taking actions that will lead them to become very wealthy by the time they retire. They will accumulate assets that will produce large amounts of income, and they may be in a higher tax bracket when they reach retirement age than they are now. In fact, they are likely to enter a higher tax bracket in just a few years as a result of their opportunistic action on the income front. If their plans are realized, then they are wise to pay taxes now while they are in a lower income bracket, and to enjoy tax-free distributions when they retire as far wealthier and higher-income individuals.

The Roth IRA is a far superior alternative to the 401(k) for those aspiring to early financial freedom but currently earn a median income or lower. It is most effective for those who believe they will manage their wealth well and become increasingly wealthy after reaching early financial freedom. This is very likely if one has intentions to learn a new skill, work part-time to stay busy, or to start businesses after leaving wage paying work.

This is likely a better option for those who really want to hustle toward early financial freedom. If you have the drive, hustle, and discipline to achieve a state of financial independence very early in life, then you are likely to continue to build wealth even after you retire from wage-paying work. You are going to keep a lifelong watchful eye on your investments, and will probably have a perpetual surplus of wealth and income to be reinvested.

Reaching a state of financial independence for someone like this is simply the start of becoming exceptionally wealthy. The game gets easier, not harder, as you progress through the levels, so long as you achieve early financial freedom early enough in life and decide to do something at least marginally productive with your free time.

As a result, it would be foolish to contribute too much to a 401(k) or traditional IRA, when you know that this money could grow tax free in a Roth, again, assuming you're currently in a lower tax bracket and expect to be in a higher tax bracket at retirement.

Obviously, the goal should be to put yourself in a position where you earn too much to be eligible to contribute to a Roth. (You are ineligible to contribute to a Roth IRA if you earn over $132,000 for individuals, and over $194,000 for married couples—note that these rates are as of 2016). But, while eligible, it can make sense to contribute to a Roth IRA .

Note: if you are a high earner and would still like to contribute to a Roth IRA, note that some companies offer a "Roth 401(k)" which you may usually contribute to regardless of income. Note also that you are often able to roll over funds from a traditional IRA to a Roth. This will involve paying taxes, and is a relatively complex process that we will not go over here. If you make too much money to contribute to a Roth IRA, you have a good problem, and should start self-educating about the conversion process, or hire a professional.

Several Reasonable Approaches to Retirement Accounts for the Aspiring Early Retiree

There are three keys to consider when investing in retirement accounts. First, make sure that you are *building sufficient wealth outside your retirement account and home equity to keep you on target for attaining early financial freedom.*

Second, note the fees. IRA and 401(k) providers are notorious for charging annual fees, which, when combined with the fees charged by the funds themselves, can result in total fees of up to 1.5 percent of the account balance. Chapter 9 discusses fees, and why investing in *index funds* and other low cost funds is so advantageous for this reason. Read that section and then choose a plan or fund with the fee structure carefully considered. If you are contributing through your employer's 401(k), understand that the fees can significantly reduce your returns. Contribute, but plan to roll over your account to something with lower fees as soon as practical (likely after you leave the company).

Thirdly, take advantage of employer matches. Here is an example of how the employer match can be a big benefit:

> *Allison earns $75,000 per year. She contributes 5 percent of her salary ($3750) toward her retirement through her company's 401(k) plan, and her company matches 50 percent of her contribution ($1875), up to 5 percent of her salary. Her total combined 401(k) balance is now $5625, and she invests this in the lowest cost index fund available in her plan.*

Well this is a no-brainer, right? Allison's company is matching her 401(k) contribution and that's basically free money for Allison, right? The short answer here is that, yes, Allison probably should take the match. There are a couple of considerations, discussed below, but in this case, it's hard to make a case against this strategy.

The first consideration: What are the terms of the match? Suppose Allison's company "vests" their 401(k) matching contributions, such that Allison forfeits all or a portion of that matching amount if she leaves the company before let's say four years. If Allison desires to leave the company to pursue an opportunity to scale her income, the money she would lose due to this "vesting" schedule becomes a bit of a trap, making her think twice about moving on to a different career with better prospects. On the other hand, if Allison has already been at the company for many years, she might find her match vests immediately. Allison would be wise to take the match from her employer and be grateful for the opportunity to receive one.

The vesting schedule is a retention tool used by companies. They don't want to pay Allison any more than they have to, but they don't want her to leave either. So, they vest their matching 401(k) contributions so that Allison is incentivized to wait it out just a few more years until her contributions are fully vested. Allison should keep in mind that unvested money isn't yet hers. She shouldn't forgo opportunities for fear of losing a small amount of unvested matches. Of course, if Allison has already been at the company for many years, then her 401(k) match may vest immediately, allowing her gain the full benefit of the matching funds even if she leaves for greener pastures.

If you believe that sticking it out for the next few years in your current line of work isn't the most impactful way for you to increase your income, then you will likely want to pounce on a better opportunity as soon as possible. In this case, it makes no sense to invest expecting anything more than the match that will be immediately vested. Don't dwell on the unvested portion. The loss of the unvested portion of the match pales in comparison to the opportunities that other employers may offer you to increase your *usable net worth.*

The second consideration is the amount of the match. In the example we used, Allison's match was 50 percent. Some companies match all of the contributions, and some match much less than the employee's contribution.

The third consideration is in an analysis of the fees and costs associated with your 401(k) plan. Some plans charge fees for the assets under management, and then offer high-fee mutual funds as the only options for employees. Often, investments offered through a 401(k) provider will result in total fees over 1 percent, which can make a huge difference in an investment that's supposed to compound over thirty years. To give you some perspective, you can invest in similar index funds through taxable investment account with fees of less than 0.05 percent—a percentage so small that it's inconsequential. Over the life of the investment, large fees can have a significant impact on overall returns.

Given those three considerations, there several ways to deal with the money in your retirement accounts (specifically the 401(k)) that align with the goal of achieving early financial freedom. Below, find a list of five strategies that can be used to transform retirement accounts from false assets to real ones.

Strategy #1: Use Your 401(k) Balance as a Hedge Against Your Current Savings Plan

If you have a comfortable, high paying job, at or above that $100,000 per year mark, and plan to have multiple years of lower income after retirement, then maxing out your 401(k) contributions now, while earning income in a high marginal tax bracket, is a simple way to build net worth that you can use to provide a large cushion to secure your financial position in old age. While it will not help you achieve early financial freedom, it may be nice to know you have some steadily growing funds that will be available later in life.

This is because the 401(k) will lower your tax payments today, and you can allow the gains to compound tax-deferred. If you achieve financial independence *outside* of needing this 401(k), you will get a nice boost when you hit "real" retirement age and can access the money in that account, which obviously isn't a bad thing.

If you are fortunate enough to be able to max out your 401(k) contributions, while at the same time building an even larger amount of usable net worth, you might feel comfortable retiring on a smaller amount of cash flow from your real assets than if you did not have the 401(k) funds there to buttress your retirement.

Strategy #2: Roth Conversion

The Roth conversion strategy is a great option for those with money in a 401(k) or other pre-tax retirement account looking to access that money early. It works well in years after early financial freedom is achieved, where one earns very little income or is in a lower tax bracket. For example, suppose that an individual earned a high income of over $100,000, contributed money to a 401(k), and then left wage paying work.

After leaving wage paying work, his income might be in a lower tax bracket. This might be a good time to convert the money in his 401(k) to a Roth. Again, it's advantageous to do this in a year where you are in a lower tax bracket, so those conversion taxes are minimized.

At this point, you will have moved the money into the Roth IRA. Normally, you can withdraw Roth IRA *contributions* immediately (but not *gains*). Please note, however, that if you take advantage of this Roth IRA "conversion" loophole, you generally need to wait five years to withdraw contributions penalty free.

The advantage to this tactic is that depending on your age it can allow you to access your retirement accounts much earlier than you might otherwise be able to. It also allows you to take advantage of years where you have little taxable income efficiently, and allows you to move money from a tax-deferred retirement plan to one that grows tax-free.

On the other hand, the Roth conversion makes little sense in years when you earn a large income. So, this strategy is really only advantageous to those who want to retire on a very low investment income.

Strategy #3: Maximize a Roth IRA

Roth IRA's are great for two primary reasons. First, the gains are tax-free. Second, you can withdraw contributions (but not gains) penalty free. It can be a great idea to make the maximum annual contribution to a Roth IRA if you are eligible—assuming you intend to withdraw your contributions to fund early financial freedom. The negligible downside to a Roth IRA is that you can't withdraw investment *gains* tax and penalty free until you turn fifty-nine and a half.

This plan is great if you expect to own businesses and investments that will compound over time to put you into the top percentiles of income late in life. Put yourself in a position to contribute the maximum amount to a Roth IRA and still save a large amount outside it.

Strategy #4: Roll Over Your IRA into a Self-directed Plan

As an additional option, there are self-directed IRA options that allow folks to not only invest in stocks, bonds, and mutual funds, but also things like real estate, private notes, private investments, and other types of alternative investments. The obvious advantage to this approach is you get to take much more control over your investments, and that you get to use your money to perhaps invest in things that you are little bit more familiar with or have more control over.

The disadvantage is that you are going to layer in a lot of complexity, and often-substantial fees for the privilege of accessing new investments with your account. Typically speaking, a self-directed IRA isn't a good bet for someone without a large 401(k) who just wants to invest in index funds, as you can probably invest in those index funds using a more traditional IRA company to do so at lower total cost. Using a self-directed IRA may make sense if you want to invest in alternative investments using retirement funds, have a substantial amount in your plan, and believe that you can achieve significantly higher returns over a long period of time than a corresponding investment in index funds.

Someone who wants to attain early financial freedom and then go on and build a profitable business at some point in the future, for example, might *roll over* a portion of her 401(k) account into a self-directed IRA. She could then use the money in the self-directed plan to invest in assets she is familiar with or in investments made accessible because of her professional or business activities and through their network.

Furthermore, many 401(k) accounts allow an employee to borrow a portion of the fund balance. A real estate investor might decide to borrow against her 401(k) account balance, paying her account interest instead of a third party. It might also make sense to buy more real estate with a self-directed 401(k), as that real estate might be under the investor's guidance and therefore produce better returns than some 401(k) plans.

Strategy #5: Substantially Equal Periodic Payments

It's possible to access the money in an IRA penalty-free before retirement, if the money is taken in the form of a substantially equal periodic payment (SEPP).

If you have money in an IRA and want to access it before retirement age, you can take a portion out every year. Although the distributions are generally still taxable, the SEPP is designed to protect you from early distribution penalties. There are several IRS-approved calculation methods, including fixed amortization method, fixed annuitization method, as well as required minimum distribution (RMD) method. With the SEPP, you are essentially deciding to take out similar amounts of distributions from your IRA each year. One of the downsides is that once the SEPP is started, you must take out a similar retirement distribution amount each year from your IRA whether you need that money or not. You are only able to stop the distribution schedule once five years have passed or you have reached age fifty-nine and a half, whichever is longer. So, if you start a SEPP schedule and in year two or three decide you don't need any money from retirement accounts that year, you would still be required to take those funds out and pay taxes on that money.

This may be a viable choice for folks who want to get at least some access to their retirement accounts before retirement age, and use them to supplement their income generated by after-tax investments.

Conclusion

Why spend all this time on retirement accounts, when we earlier describe them as false assets? The answer is that retirement accounts *can* be usable net worth, if you *intend* to use them to expedite your early retirement or greatly increase your present-day decision-making. There are several ways described herein to take advantage of these accounts to defer or reduce taxes over time, and to advantageously build wealth.

The problem, however, is that if *most* of your wealth is in retirement accounts, then you may be unwilling or unable to use it in pursuit of *early* financial freedom. This kind of wealth building provides little financial runway, and fails to empower decision-making that might hasten early financial freedom. If all or most of your saving is going to a retirement account, begin making changes. Begin saving most of your wealth *after* tax, and using it to generate income that can be used toward early financial freedom penalty-free. But, do not entirely forgo the benefits of retirement accounts either. Take advantage of employer matches and Roth IRAs. Invest in retirement accounts with a proper plan in place, such that they can be harnessed early to sustain a lifetime of financial freedom both now, and later in life.

DAILY TIME LOG

My Goals:

1) _____

2) _____

3) _____

Three things I am grateful for today:

Gratitude 1:_____

Gratitude 2:_____

Gratitude 3:_____

Three important people I will reach out to today are:

Person 1: _____

Person 2: _____

Person 3: _____

My five goal related actions:

Action 1: _____

Action 2: _____

Action 3: _____

Action 4: _____

Action 5: _____

Other chores and tasks necessary to maintaining my life:

Task 1: _____

Task 2: _____

Task 3: _____

Task 4: _____

Task 5: _____

My thirty minutes to one hour of learning today included the following:

_____

_____

Describe the physical activity done today: _____

Describe the healthy food eaten today: _____

Write down the important actions completed in each of the following time blocks.

Early Morning (before 9:00 am):

Late AM (9:00am to 12:00 pm):

Early PM (12:00p to 2:30 pm):

Late PM (2:30pm to 5:00 pm):

Early Evening (5:00pm to 7:30 pm):

Late Evening (after 7:30 pm):

Any reflections on the day: Journal for five minutes and reflect on the day. Plan out activities for the next day.

_____

_____

_____

_____

_____

_____

_____

_____

_____

_____

_____

_____

WEEKLY OUTLINE

My Quarterly Objectives:

1) _____

2) _____

3) _____

Actions needed to accomplish quarterly objectives:

- Weekly actions related to quarterly objective #1
  - _____
  - _____
  - _____

- Weekly actions related to quarterly objective #2
  - _____
  - _____
  - _____

- Weekly actions related to quarterly objective #3
  - _____
  - _____
  - _____

My Top Focuses (sample):

- Important people I need to prioritize this week
- Learning and educational priority for the week
- Plan out a healthy diet for at least three meals per day each day this week
- Exercise intensely at least five days this week

Additional things to work toward if time allows (sample):

1) Complete daily log seven days this week
2) Begin tracking my finances using Mint or Personal Capital
3) Bike to work four out of five weekdays
4) Look for apartment or house hack that is close to work
5) Consider a new line of work that offers the opportunity to scale
6) Buy my first shares of a low cost index fund
7) Listen to a podcast on real estate investing
8) Meet three people who have achieved early financial freedom

QUARTERLY PLAN

My Quarterly Plan:

1) _____

2) _____

3) _____

Weekly Outline:

Week #1 plan:
    Objective related to Goal #1
    Objective related to Goal #2
    Objective related to Goal #3

Week #2 plan:
    Objective related to Goal #1
    Objective related to Goal #2
    Objective related to Goal #3

Week #3 plan:
    Objective related to Goal #1
    Objective related to Goal #2
    Objective related to Goal #3

Week #4 plan:
    Objective related to Goal #1
    Objective related to Goal #2
    Objective related to Goal #3

Week #5 plan:
    Objective related to Goal #1
    Objective related to Goal #2
    Objective related to Goal #3

Week #6 plan:
    Objective related to Goal #1
    Objective related to Goal #2
    Objective related to Goal #3

Week #7 plan:
    Objective related to Goal #1
    Objective related to Goal #2
    Objective related to Goal #3

Week #8 plan:
    Objective related to Goal #1
    Objective related to Goal #2
    Objective related to Goal #3

Week #9 plan:
    Objective related to Goal #1
    Objective related to Goal #2
    Objective related to Goal #3

Week #10 plan:
    Objective related to Goal #1
    Objective related to Goal #2
    Objective related to Goal #3

Week #11 plan:
    Objective related to Goal #1
    Objective related to Goal #2
    Objective related to Goal #3

Week #12 plan:
    Objective related to Goal #1
    Objective related to Goal #2
    Objective related to Goal #3

YEAR LONG RESOLUTIONS

My Goals:

1) _____
2) _____
3) _____

12 Accomplishments to satisfy by the end of the year:

1) Accomplishment for Goal #1 (Q1): _____
2) Accomplishment for Goal #1 (Q2): _____
3) Accomplishment for Goal #1 (Q3): _____
4) Accomplishment for Goal #1 (Q4): _____
5) Accomplishment for Goal #2 (Q1): _____
6) Accomplishment for Goal #2 (Q2): _____
7) Accomplishment for Goal #2 (Q3): _____
8) Accomplishment for Goal #2 (Q4): _____
9) Accomplishment for Goal #3 (Q1): _____
10) Accomplishment for Goal #3 (Q2): _____
11) Accomplishment for Goal #3 (Q3): _____
12) Accomplishment for Goal #3 (Q4): _____

12 Habits to form this year:

- Habit #1: _____
- Habit #2: _____
- Habit #3: _____
- Habit #4: _____
- Habit #5: _____
- Habit #6: _____
- Habit #7: _____
- Habit #8: _____
- Habit #9: _____
- Habit #10: _____
- Habit #11: _____
- Habit #12: _____

Acknowledgments

This book is dedicated to my loving and wonderful mother, Lynne Trench. It's through her support and guidance that I've been able to make it through many of life's challenges. Thank you for everything, Mom. In addition, I would like to thank Randy Trench for his support and expertise, as a parent, mentor, and writing coach. I'd like to thank Kimberly Peticolas for her organization and management of the publishing process. I'd like to thank Daniel Friedman for his patience and thoughtful review and feedback. I'd like to thank Walker Hinshaw for his friendship, partnership, and his help in guiding my thought process. I'd like to thank Virginia Hornblower for her support throughout the process, her help with my writing, and for our relationship. I'd like to thank Ellie at Pressque for her copious edits and assistance through the copyediting process. I'd like to thank Amanda Han and Brandon Hall for their contributions to the section on Retirement Accounts.

I'd like to thank the entire BiggerPockets team, with a special acknowledgement to Joshua Dorkin, Brandon Turner, Allison Leung, and Jarrod Jamison for their specific assistance throughout the writing and book creation process.

I'd also like to thank all of the people who gave me feedback on my book, including Kirby-Nicole Tracy Gilliam, Zack Goldman, Tim Coil, James McCabe, Benjamin Allen, Vignesh Swaminathan, and Rusty Trench.

MORE FROM BIGGERPOCKETS

If you enjoyed this book, we hope you'll take a moment to check out some of the other great books BiggerPockets Publishing offers. BiggerPockets is the real estate investing social network, marketplace, and information hub, designed to help make you a smarter real estate investor through podcasts, blog posts, videos, forums, files, and more. Sign up today—it's free! www.BiggerPockets.com

Be sure to also read:

The Book on Rental Property Investing *By Brandon Turner*

The Book on Rental Property Investing, written by real estate investor and co-host of the BiggerPockets Podcast Brandon Turner, contains nearly 400 pages of in-depth advice and strategies for building wealth through rental properties. You'll learn how to build an achievable plan, find incredible deals, pay for your rentals, and much, more more!

The Book on Managing Rental Properties

By Brandon & Heather Turner

No matter how great you are at finding good rental property deals, you could lose everything if you don't manage your properties correctly! But being a landlord doesn't have to mean middle-of-the-night phone calls, costly evictions, or daily frustrations with ungrateful tenants. Being a landlord can actually be fun IF you do it right.

The Book on Investing in Real Estate with No (and Low) Money Downs By *Brandon Turner*

Is a lack of money holding you back from real estate success? It doesn't have to! In this groundbreaking book from Brandon Turner, author of *The Book on Rental Property Investing*, you'll discover numerous strategies a real estate investor can use to buy real estate using other people's money. You'll learn the top strategies that savvy investors are using to buy, rent, flip, wholesale properties at scale!

The Book on Tax Strategies for the Savvy Real Estate Investor By *Amanda Han & Matthew MacFarland*

Taxes! Boring and irritating, right?

Perhaps. But if you want to succeed in real estate, your tax strategy will play a HUGE role in how fast you grow. A great tax strategy can save you thousands of dollars a year—and a bad strategy could land you in legal trouble. *The Book on Tax Strategies for the Savvy Real Estate Investor* will help you deduct more, invest smarter, and pay far less to the IRS!

The Book on Flipping Houses & The Book on Estimating Rehab Costs By *J. Scott*

The Book on Flipping Houses, contains more than 300 pages of detailed, step-by-step training perfect for both the complete newbie and the seasoned pro. *The Book on Estimating Rehab Costs* pulls back the curtain on the rehab process to show you not only the cost ranges and details associated with every aspect of a rehab, but also the framework and methodology for estimating rehab costs.